Body
for
LIFE

SUCCESS
Journal

Body
for
LIFE

SUCCESS
Journal

Bill Phillips

HarperCollins*Publishers*

HarperCollins books may be purchased for educational, business, or sales promotional use. For information, please write: Special Markets Department, HarperCollins Publishers Inc., 10 East 53rd Street, New York, NY 10022.

The Body-*for*-LIFE Program is intended for healthy adults, age 18 and over. This book is solely for informational and educational purposes and is not medical advice. Please consult a medical or health professional before you begin any new exercise, nutrition, or supplementation program, or if you have questions about your health. Some of the individuals featured in this book were competing for cash and prizes in an EAS-sponsored shape-up challenge and have received consideration from EAS. They achieved extraordinary results; there are no "typical" results. Their success stories represent extraordinary examples of what can be accomplished through an integrated system of exercise and nutrition. As individuals differ, their results will differ, even when using the same program.

FIRST EDITION

Designed by Craig Korn

Produced by Michael Sitzman

ISBN 0-06-051559-7

Printed in China

02 03 04 05 06 ❖/TOP 10 9 8 7 6 5 4 3 2 1

"You will be as successful as you plan to be!"

I am so happy and excited to be sharing this new book with you! I feel very confident this *Success Journal* will help you transform your body and improve your quality of life. Whether you've completed the Body-*for*-LIFE Program before and are looking to take your results to the next level, or if this will be your first successful transformation, I know this book will help you achieve your goals.

Having had the opportunity to read and review literally tens of thousands of success stories over the past three years, I have learned that planning and recording your workouts, nutrition, and Body-*for*-LIFE mindset are perhaps *the* most important exercises you can do to ensure your success.

This *Success Journal* will help you apply all of the principles you learned by reading my original Body-*for*-LIFE book. It will guide you, day by day, step by step, through the entire 12-week Program. I have carefully designed each and every page of this book to remove virtually all of the guesswork. I will be with you every step of the way and so will other people who have successfully completed the Program. Each and every day we will support you, encourage you, and help you stay focused and inspired.

When you finish this *Success Journal*, it will document *your* success story. However, the real reward will be your new, transformed body and your clear, empowered mindset!

Before we go any further, please pick up a ballpoint pen or pencil and answer this very important question: *Have you made the decision to make a change?*

☑ **Yes!** I'm ready to make a change for the better!

❑ No. I'm *not* happy with the way I am, but I'm determined to stay that way.

If you answered "Yes!" to the question above, congratulations! You've taken the first step toward transforming your Body-*for*-LIFE. Please turn the page and let's continue this journey together!

On the right-facing page is an example of what I call a "Dream List." This is a very important "exercise" to complete before you actually begin the Body-*for*-LIFE workouts and nutrition method.

To complete this exercise, what you do is simply tap into your imagination and just write down any words and phrases that come to mind when you think about successfully completing this 12-week Program. There's no right or wrong way to do this exercise. Don't "overthink" it—just follow your heart. Be open, honest, and spontaneous. The images that come to mind quickly, spark positive emotions, and give you inspiration are your *dreams*. When you imagine them actually happening, you'll feel more energy.

You'll notice in the example to the right that through this process of exploring ideas you will see a pattern of connected images that form a bigger picture—a picture of a healthy, energetic new you!

One of the reasons this exercise is so important is that by "free styling" and bringing some of your subconscious health and fitness dreams to the surface, you'll be able to create very meaningful goals that are unique to you.

It's very important to understand the difference between dreams and goals. Dreams are things you wish for—things you enjoy thinking about but don't really know when or if they'll happen. Goals, on the other hand, are *specific* things you have decided you will accomplish within a clearly defined period of time. For example, "Someday I'm going to get in great shape" is a dream. "Within 12 weeks, I *will* lose 20 pounds of fat" is a goal. Notice that goals can be measured, which allow you to *know* that you've achieved them.

Here's another important point: Your goals come from your dreams. Inspiring dreams will give you energy to set inspiring goals, which, in turn, will help you make changes for the better and transform your body and life.

After you finish your Dream List, read it over again and let it serve as the inspiration for setting *your* clear-cut 12-week goals.

Please write down any and all hopes, wishes, and dreams that you would like to see come true as a result of completing this 12-week Body-*for*-LIFE Program.

Help Others!

Be a ~~good~~ great parent!

Transform!

Build muscle!

☺

BE HAPPY!

LESS STRESS!

Be strong!

Healthy Heart!

LOOK YOUNGER! FEEL YOUNGER!

ENERGY!!!!

Skiing, Golfing, Running!

Lose fat!

SUCCESS!

CONFIDENT!

Slender waist!

Feel good about myself!

Feel like myself again!

Live a long life!

LOOK GREAT ON THE BEACH IN MAUI!

On the right-facing page, you first see an example of 5 specific 12-week goals. You develop these goals from your Dream List. For example, if you wrote down "gain muscle" and "lose fat" on your Dream List, you might write the following goals: "Within 12 weeks, I *will* gain 5 pounds of muscle!" And "Within 12 weeks, I *will* lose 20 pounds of fat!" By composing sentences like these, by defining and stating your wish, and by setting a deadline (within 12 weeks), you'll be transforming your dreams into *goals*. Once you clarify your goals, be sure to read them first thing in the morning and again at night.

Here's the next exercise you'll see on the right-facing page: Identify your *reasons* for achieving your 12-week goals. What I've discovered is that the more clear you are about *why* those goals are important to you, the more likely it is you'll succeed. It's not complicated at all to identify reasons for making changes to improve your health and fitness. There are countless reasons for wanting to become healthier, stronger, and more energetic. Be sure to write down three that have meaning to you. And please read your reasons every time you review your goals.

The next exercise on the right-facing page is called Transforming Patterns of Action. To complete this exercise, you identify three habits you have now, which you'll need to transform in order for you to move forward and become a success. For example, if one of your goals is to lose 20 pounds of fat within 12 weeks, it's very likely you will need to begin carefully planning nutritious meals, instead of just eating carelessly. I've discovered the best way to develop new, healthy habits is to identify ones that are not working for you and pretty much do the opposite.

By clearly stating your goals, identifying reasons why those goals are important to you, and by writing down three old, "unauthorized" patterns of action and three new, effective ones, you're "Crossing the Abyss," which I discussed in detail in Part II of the Body-*for*-LIFE book (page 21). Be sure to review this section of the book carefully before you begin this 12-week Body-*for*-LIFE Program.

Body-*for*-LIFE 12-Week Goals

**Please write down 5 specific goals you will achieve
over the course of your 12-week Program.**

1 Within 12 weeks, I will lose 20 lbs of bodyfat!

2 Within 12 weeks, I will gain 5 lbs of muscle!

3 Within 12 weeks, I will reduce my cholesterol to below 200!

4 Within 12 weeks, I will increase my strength by at least 10%!

5 Within 12 weeks, I will help at least 2 other people begin Body-for-LIFE!

Body-*for*-LIFE Reasons

**Please write down 3 reasons why you have
decided to achieve your 12-week goals.**

1 I want to be healthy!

2 I want to look and feel great!

3 I want to be a positive example and an inspiration to others!

Body-*for*-LIFE Transforming Patterns of Action

**Please write down 3 patterns of action you need to transform
in order to successfully achieve your 12-week goals.**

1 **Old Pattern:** Eating carelessly.

New Pattern: Planning and eating 6 nutritious meals daily.

2 **Old Pattern:** Not working out regularly.

New Pattern: Planning and performing intense workouts 6 days a week.

3 **Old Pattern:** Not setting goals for my health and fitness.

New Pattern: Setting and focusing on important health and fitness goals!

On the right-facing page, you see examples of three more important Body-*for*-LIFE exercises. The first one is called The Power Mindset. This exercise helps you focus on and prioritize your daily Body-*for*-LIFE activities. You see, in order to experience an extraordinary transformation in just 12 weeks, you need to make progress every day. And by simply deciding what 5 things you can do tomorrow to move forward in the direction of your 12-week goals, you will stay on course and remain focused.

Also on this page is the Universal Law of Reciprocation exercise, which I wrote about in the Body-*for*-LIFE book (page 106). In order to make the successful transformation you've decided to make, you *will* need support and encouragement. And the best way to receive is to *give*. This simple exercise creates immediate results that will increase your energy and confidence. When you say something as simple as, "I appreciate your support!" or "Good work!" you not only give someone else a boost, but according to the Universal Law of Reciprocation, you will *receive* more positive energy than you give.

Both of these exercises should be planned during your evening journaling session. During the course of the next day, or your *next* evening journaling session, review what you planned to do, and if you followed your plan, write "Success!" in the Actual column. If you did not achieve your daily goal, write "Setback," and be sure to try harder tomorrow.

The next mindset exercise on the right-facing page is Focus on Progress, Not Perfection. You should complete this exercise *only* during your evening journaling session. What you'll do here is reflect on your day and write down three things you did very well that helped you move forward. This exercise gives you positive reinforcement and helps you build momentum, because you're giving yourself credit where credit is due. When you look for three things you've done *right* that day, you'll find them! Your final assignment is to identify just one thing you can do *even better* tomorrow than you did today.

Body-*for*-LIFE The Power Mindset

Please write down 5 things you can do between now and this time tomorrow that will help you move forward in the direction of your 12-week goals.

	PLAN	ACTUAL
1	Work out intensely tomorrow morning and hit my high points!	Success!
2	Plan my nutrition and stick with my plan.	Success!
3	Read my 12-week goals and imagine achieving them!	Setback
4	Do not eat junk food or candy!	Success!
5	Drink 10 glasses of water.	Success!

Body-*for*-LIFE The Universal Law of Reciprocation

Please write down 2 things you can do between now and this time tomorrow to support and encourage others.

	PLAN	ACTUAL
1	Visit BodyforLIFE.com and encourage others!	Success!
2	Write an encouraging note to my partner at work!	Success!

Body-*for*-LIFE Focus on Progress, Not Perfection

Please write down 3 things you did very well today that helped you move toward the achievement of your 12-week goals.

1	I worked out intensely this morning and hit my high points!
2	I encouraged others!
3	I wrote in my Success Journal this morning and tonight!

Please write down one thing you will do even better tomorrow.

1	I will invest more time imagining my goals being achieved!

Notes:

On the right-facing page is an example of how to plan and record your Body-*for*-LIFE nutrition method. Please notice that all you need to do here is write down *what* you plan to eat and *when*. Be sure to plan your meals for the coming day the night before. Throughout the day, simply record what you actually ate and when. This is another very simple, but powerful, journaling technique that will help ensure your success.

Remember, quality nutrition is just as important as intense exercise. (Exercise is the *spark*. Nutrition is the *fuel*. Without *both*, there can be no flame—no results.) As soon as you start exercising intensely, you *must* begin eating the right way; you must start consistently feeding your body what it needs to re-create itself, so you can enjoy rapid and rewarding progress.

To help adopt this new pattern of eating—of *intentionally* feeding your body the nutrients it needs to re-create itself—please make sure your cupboards and refrigerator are stocked with authorized foods (see the list of "Authorized Foods" on page 83 of Body-*for*-LIFE). I'll say it yet again: If you fail to plan, you're planning to fail. And planning your meals requires that you *also* plan your grocery shopping. Stock up *only* on quality sources of protein, carbohydrates, fruits, vegetables, and other essentials.

For detailed information and numerous examples of authorized meals, please carefully review Part V (beginning on page 81) of your Body-*for*-LIFE book. And please keep these important points in mind as you move forward: Eat six small meals a day, one every two to three hours; eat a portion (a portion is the amount of an authorized food approximately the size of the palm of your hand) of protein and carbohydrates with each meal; add a portion of vegetables to at least two meals daily; consume one tablespoon of unsaturated oil daily or three portions of salmon per week; drink at least 10 cups of water a day; use a nutrition shake like Myoplex,™ if necessary, to make sure you're consuming optimal levels of nutrients; and once a week, on your free day, eat *whatever* you want.

Body-*for*-LIFE   The Eating-*for*-LIFE Method™

	PLAN		ACTUAL	
Meal 1	Egg Beater Omelette	**Meal 1**	Egg Beater Omelette	
8:00 ☑a.m. ☐p.m.	Whole wheat toast	8:00 ☑a.m. ☐p.m.	Whole wheat toast	
	1 cup coffee		1 cup coffee	
	2 cups water		2 cups water	
Meal 2	Chocolate Myoplex shake	**Meal 2**	Chocolate Myoplex shake	
10:00 ☑a.m. ☐p.m.	made with 2 cups water	10:00 ☑a.m. ☐p.m.	made with 2 cups water	
Meal 3	Grilled chicken breast	**Meal 3**	Grilled chicken breast	
12:00 ☐a.m. ☑p.m.	Baked potato	12:00 ☐a.m. ☑p.m.	Baked potato	
	Steamed spinach		Steamed spinach	
	2 cups water		2 cups water	
Meal 4	Low-fat cottage cheese	**Meal 4**	Low-fat cottage cheese	
3:00 ☐a.m. ☑p.m.	1 apple	3:00 ☐a.m. ☑p.m.	1 apple	
	2 cups water		2 cups water	
Meal 5	Grilled salmon	**Meal 5**	Grilled salmon	
6:00 ☐a.m. ☑p.m.	Brown rice	6:10 ☐a.m. ☑p.m.	Brown rice	
	Steamed broccoli		Steamed broccoli	
	2 cups water		2 cups water	
Meal 6	Myoplex pudding	**Meal 6**	Myoplex pudding	
9:00 ☐a.m. ☑p.m.	1 cup water	9:15 ☐a.m. ☑p.m.	1 cup water	

Notes: –I feel great today. Good energy and strong!

✳ –Wanted to have pizza tonight but looked at my before picture and
decided to stick with my plan!! I am so glad I did! ☺

–I need to pick up brown rice, vegetables, fruit and fresh fish when I go
grocery shopping this weekend.

On the right-facing page is an example of how to plan *and* record your Body-*for*-LIFE workouts. This particular example is of an upper body workout. Please notice that I've organized and structured the exercise session for you. All you need to plan are these four things: What time you'll *start* your workout; what time you plan to *finish* it; what *exercises* you'll do; and the *weights* you plan to lift. That's it. There's nothing complicated about it! And once you get the hang of it, your planning sessions will require only a few minutes each night. Notice that in addition to planning, you also need to *record* what you actually do—what weights you lift and what intensity level you hit. You can record your workout during your exercise session or right after it. You'll learn that this requires only a few minutes as well.

Remember that you weight train, intensely, for no more than 46 minutes, 3 times per week: Monday, Wednesday, and Friday. You perform two exercises for each major muscle group of the upper and lower body.

You also perform 20 minutes of aerobic exercise, first thing in the morning, on an empty stomach, 3 times per week: Tuesday, Thursday, and Saturday. And you plan and record these workouts, too.

Through your records, you can clearly see the path you're on. If you're not transforming as rapidly as you would like, you can go back and troubleshoot, with precision. Are you hitting the appropriate intensity levels? Are you lifting too much or not enough weight? These are the types of questions you'll be able to answer when you keep a detailed journal.

Be sure to review Part IV (beginning on page 55) of your Body-*for*-LIFE book to remind yourself of the workout principles, especially the High Point Technique. And remember that you can find detailed instructions, including photographs, of how to do the 36 best, basic weight-lifting exercises beginning on page 135 of your Body-*for*-LIFE book. You can also find video exercise demonstrations on www.BodyforLIFE.com.

Body-*for*-LIFE — Upper Body Workout

Intensity Pattern

	PLAN	ACTUAL
Planned Start Time: 6:05		Actual Start Time: 6:10
Planned End Time: 6:51		Actual End Time: 6:55
Time to Complete: 46 Minutes		Time to Complete: 45 Minutes

Upper Body Muscle Groups	Exercise	Reps	Weight (lbs)	Minutes Between Sets	Intensity Level	Reps	Weight (lbs)	Minutes Between Sets	Intensity Level
Chest	Dumbbell Bench Press	12	40	1	5	12	40	1	5
	Dumbbell Bench Press	10	50	1	6	10	50	1	6
	Dumbbell Bench Press	8	60	1	7	8	60	1	7
	Dumbbell Bench Press	6	70	1	8	6	70	1	8
High Point	Dumbbell Bench Press	12	60	0	9	12	60	0	9
	Dumbbell Flyes	12	40	2	10	12	40	2	10!
Shoulders	Seated Dumbbell Press	12	30	1	5	12	30	1	5
	Seated Dumbbell Press	10	40	1	6	10	40	1	6
	Seated Dumbbell Press	8	45	1	7	8	45	1	7
	Seated Dumbbell Press	6	50	1	8	6	50	1	8
High Point	Seated Dumbbell Press	12	45	0	9	12	45	0	9
	Side Raises	12	10	2	10	12	10	2	9
Back	Dumbbell Rows	12	40	1	5	12	40	1	5
	Dumbbell Rows	10	50	1	6	10	50	1	6
	Dumbbell Rows	8	60	1	7	8	60	1	7
	Dumbbell Rows	6	70	1	8	6	70	1	8
High Point	Dumbbell Rows	12	60	0	9	12	60	0	9
	Dumbbell Pullovers	12	70	2	10	12	70	2	9
Triceps	Seated Dumbbell Extensions	12	50	1	5	12	50	1	5
	Seated Dumbbell Extensions	10	60	1	6	10	60	1	6
	Seated Dumbbell Extensions	8	70	1	7	8	70	1	7
	Seated Dumbbell Extensions	6	80	1	8	6	80	1	8
High Point	Seated Dumbbell Extensions	12	70	0	9	12	70	0	9
	Lying Triceps Extensions	12	20	2	10	12	20	2	10

At this point, you should be 37 minutes into your upper body workout and have 9 minutes to go.

Biceps	Seated Dumbbell Curls	12	25	1	5	12	25	1	5
	Seated Dumbbell Curls	10	30	1	6	10	30	1	6
	Seated Dumbbell Curls	8	35	1	7	8	35	1	7
	Seated Dumbbell Curls	6	40	1	8	6	40	1	8
High Point	Seated Dumbbell Curls	12	35	0	9	12	35	0	9
	Standing Dumbbell Curls	12	30	–	10	12	30	–	9

Notes: *Need to go up to 15-pound dumbbells for side raises next time. I need to increase my weight on dumbbell pullovers from 70 to 80 pounds and try harder next time. —Overall, this workout went according to plan and I felt great after I finished!*

On the right-facing page is *your* 12-week Body-*for*-LIFE schedule, which serves two primary purposes. The first is to help you plan your workouts and free days. You'll notice that I have clearly indicated what type of exercise you need to perform each day. This Program is designed to be started on a Monday, and your free day is designated as Sunday. (Your before picture should be taken on Monday, Day 1 of your Program, and your after picture should be taken on Day 84.)

The second purpose of this schedule is to help you document your success. Below is an example of how to chart your daily progress so you see the big picture developing. Use three "LIFE-lines" to indicate the successful daily completion of your workouts, proper nutrition, and mindset exercises. Specifically, a straight line across (—) is used to indicate completion of your mindset exercises; a downward slant (\ ) indicates successfully following your nutrition plan; an upward slant (/) indicates successfully performing that day's workout. Completion of all three major aspects of the Program form a star (✳). As you progress, you'll want to see more stars than x's or slashes.

In the example week below, you'll see three LIFE-lines on Day 1, which form a star, indicating the completion of that day's workout, nutrition, and mindset exercises. On Day 2, you'll notice *only* two LIFE-lines, which indicate successfully completing that day's workout and nutrition plans. What's missing is a horizontal line, which would represent the completion of that day's mindset exercise.

Week 1	Day 1 Upper Body Weight Training	Day 2 20-Minute Aerobics Solution	Day 3 Lower Body Weight Training	Day 4 20-Minute Aerobics Solution	Day 5 Upper Body Weight Training	Day 6 20-Minute Aerobics Solution	Day 7 Free Day

Documenting your success through the use of this 12-week schedule is a very important process. As the days and weeks go by, you'll be able to glance at the schedule and see your transformation developing. You'll be able to measure your progress, and you'll also become very conscious of what areas you might need to improve. Shoot for the stars and you *will* have a successful 12-week journey!

Body-*for*-LIFE | 12-Week Journey to Success

Planned Start Date: March 28/05   Planned Finish Date: _____

Actual Start Date: Mcnh 28/05   Actual Finish Date: _____

	MONDAY	TUESDAY	WEDNESDAY	THURSDAY	FRIDAY	SATURDAY	SUNDAY
Week 1	Day 1 Upper Body Weight Training	Day 2 20-Minute Aerobics Solution	Day 3 Lower Body Weight Training	Day 4 20-Minute Aerobics Solution	Day 5 Upper Body Weight Training	Day 6 20-Minute Aerobics Solution	Day 7 Free Day
Week 2	Day 8 Lower Body Weight Training	Day 9 20-Minute Aerobics Solution	Day 10 Upper Body Weight Training	Day 11 20-Minute Aerobics Solution	Day 12 Lower Body Weight Training	Day 13 20-Minute Aerobics Solution	Day 14 Free Day
Week 3	Day 15 Upper Body Weight Training	Day 16 20-Minute Aerobics Solution	Day 17 Lower Body Weight Training	Day 18 20-Minute Aerobics Solution	Day 19 Upper Body Weight Training	Day 20 20-Minute Aerobics Solution	Day 21 Free Day
Week 4	Day 22 Lower Body Weight Training	Day 23 20-Minute Aerobics Solution	Day 24 Upper Body Weight Training	Day 25 20-Minute Aerobics Solution	Day 26 Lower Body Weight Training	Day 27 20-Minute Aerobics Solution	Day 28 Free Day
Week 5	Day 29 Upper Body Weight Training	Day 30 20-Minute Aerobics Solution	Day 31 Lower Body Weight Training	Day 32 20-Minute Aerobics Solution	Day 33 Upper Body Weight Training	Day 34 20-Minute Aerobics Solution	Day 35 Free Day
Week 6	Day 36 Lower Body Weight Training	Day 37 20-Minute Aerobics Solution	Day 38 Upper Body Weight Training	Day 39 20-Minute Aerobics Solution	Day 40 Lower Body Weight Training	Day 41 20-Minute Aerobics Solution	Day 42 Free Day
Week 7	Day 43 Upper Body Weight Training	Day 44 20-Minute Aerobics Solution	Day 45 Lower Body Weight Training	Day 46 20-Minute Aerobics Solution	Day 47 Upper Body Weight Training	Day 48 20-Minute Aerobics Solution	Day 49 Free Day
Week 8	Day 50 Lower Body Weight Training	Day 51 20-Minute Aerobics Solution	Day 52 Upper Body Weight Training	Day 53 20-Minute Aerobics Solution	Day 54 Lower Body Weight Training	Day 55 20-Minute Aerobics Solution	Day 56 Free Day
Week 9	Day 57 Upper Body Weight Training	Day 58 20-Minute Aerobics Solution	Day 59 Lower Body Weight Training	Day 60 20-Minute Aerobics Solution	Day 61 Upper Body Weight Training	Day 62 20-Minute Aerobics Solution	Day 63 Free Day
Week 10	Day 64 Lower Body Weight Training	Day 65 20-Minute Aerobics Solution	Day 66 Upper Body Weight Training	Day 67 20-Minute Aerobics Solution	Day 68 Lower Body Weight Training	Day 69 20-Minute Aerobics Solution	Day 70 Free Day
Week 11	Day 71 Upper Body Weight Training	Day 72 20-Minute Aerobics Solution	Day 73 Lower Body Weight Training	Day 74 20-Minute Aerobics Solution	Day 75 Upper Body Weight Training	Day 76 20-Minute Aerobics Solution	Day 77 Free Day
Week 12	Day 78 Lower Body Weight Training	Day 79 20-Minute Aerobics Solution	Day 80 Upper Body Weight Training	Day 81 20-Minute Aerobics Solution	Day 82 Lower Body Weight Training	Day 83 20-Minute Aerobics Solution	Day 84 Success!

Body-*for*-LIFE   Dream List

Body-*for*-LIFE   12-Week Goals

**Please write down 5 specific goals you will achieve
over the course of your 12-week Program.**

1

2

3

4

5

Body-*for*-LIFE   Reasons

**Please write down 3 reasons why you have
decided to achieve your 12-week goals.**

1

2

3

Body-*for*-LIFE   Transforming Patterns of Action

**Please write down 3 patterns of action you need to transform
in order to successfully achieve your 12-week goals.**

1   Old Pattern:

New Pattern:

2   Old Pattern:

New Pattern:

3   Old Pattern:

New Pattern:

Before Photo and Measurements

Beginning

Date: Weight: Bodyfat %:

Other:

Please take your after photo and attach it in the space below. (Double-sided tape works well.)

Success!

Date: _____   Weight: _____   Bodyfat %: _____

Other: _____

Body-*for*-LIFE Your Success Story

Your before and after photos clearly show your successful body transformation. Please write your answers to these 6 questions, *after* you have completed your 12-week Program, to reveal how you've transformed your mindset, energy, and emotions.

1 Having now successfully completed the 12-week Program, how good do you feel and how much more energy do you have compared to before?

2 To make it through all 12 weeks, you clearly had to stay focused and inspired. How did you do that?

3 What's the biggest obstacle you had to overcome in order to successfully complete your 12-week Program, and how did you do it?

4 How has your life improved by transforming your body and health?

5 Now that you have successfully completed this 12-week Body-*for*-LIFE Program, how are you going to build on your momentum and what will you achieve next?

6 If you could inspire only *one* person to follow your example and experience all the positive changes you have over the past 12 weeks, *who* would that person be; why would you choose *that* person; and *how* would you help that person succeed as you have?

Bill Phillips — Lesson-*for*-LIFE

"The plan I utilized to go from 'before' to 'after' back in 1992 has evolved into Body-*for*-LIFE."

In the Fall of 1992, I made plans to go on a Christmas vacation to the Bahamas with my girlfriend. I remember it like it was yesterday. I made our reservations on my birthday, September 23. The next day, I was imagining how much fun we would have under the sun, on the beach, and swimming in the Caribbean. The problem was I wasn't happy with the shape I was in at the time. Through careless eating, I'd gained so much fat I couldn't see any muscle definition. Although I was an expert weight trainer and had been going to the gym six days a week, I was not putting it all together. I wanted to be at my best, so I developed a new, more focused plan and set a goal of losing 20 pounds of fat and increasing my muscle definition and energy before our vacation.

I had my girlfriend take a "before" photo, which helped me clearly see the condition I was in, and on October 3, I officially started my Program. Each day I planned my workouts and nutrition. I changed the way I was eating, started training more intensely, and focused on my goals. Twelve weeks later, on December 26, 1992, I achieved my goals and hit the beach happy with how I looked. More important, I felt great! My girlfriend and I had so much fun!

In the months that followed, I showed my before and after pictures to others and shared my "success story." The response was virtually universal: "Can you help me do that?!" Ever since, I've been teaching people how to transform in as little as 12 weeks. And the plan I utilized to go from "before" to "after" back in 1992 has now evolved into this, the Body-*for*-LIFE Program.

Body-*for*-LIFE The Power Mindset

Please write down 5 things you can do between now and this time tomorrow
that will help you move forward in the direction of your 12-week goals.

	PLAN	ACTUAL
1	workout allprice few	Yes
2	BE EFFICIENT + EFFECTIVE e wn	
3	— FINANCES IN ORDER	No
4		
5		

Body-*for*-LIFE The Universal Law of Reciprocation

Please write down 2 things you can do between now and
this time tomorrow to support and encourage others.

	PLAN	ACTUAL
1	discuss BODY FOR LIFE	
2		

Body-*for*-LIFE Focus on Progress, Not Perfection

Please write down 3 things you did very well today that helped
you move toward the achievement of your 12-week goals.

1	
2	
3	

Please write down one thing you will do even better tomorrow.

1	

Notes:

Body-*for*-LIFE — The Eating-*for*-LIFE Method™

PLAN		ACTUAL	
Meal 1		**Meal 1**	
7:15 ☑a.m. ☐p.m.	phosphagen Simply protein water + apple	8:45 ☑a.m. ☐p.m.	pnrm shake + phorph + chit
Meal 2		**Meal 2**	
16:0 ☑a.m. ☐p.m.	myoplx shake	11:00 ☑a.m. ☐p.m.	nut ni chn myxl
Meal 3		**Meal 3**	
1:00 ☐a.m. ☑p.m.	tuna sandwich	☐a.m. ☐p.m.	sandwh
Meal 4		**Meal 4**	
4:00 ☐a.m. ☑p.m.	Dar	☐a.m. ☐p.m.	½ tuna
Meal 5		**Meal 5**	
7:00 ☐a.m. ☐p.m.	fish + salad	☐a.m. ☐p.m.	fish
Meal 6		**Meal 6**	
10 ☐a.m. ☑p.m.	myoplx shak	☐a.m. ☐p.m.	

Notes: phen-free x2 @ 6:00

Body-*for*-LIFE Upper Body Workout

Intensity Pattern

	PLAN				ACTUAL			
Planned Start Time: 6:05					Actual Start Time: 7:52			
Planned End Time: 7:01					Actual End Time:			
Time to Complete: 46 Minutes					Time to Complete:			

Upper Body Muscle Groups	Exercise	Reps	Weight (lbs)	Minutes Between Sets	Intensity Level	Reps	Weight (lbs)	Minutes Between Sets	Intensity Level
Chest	incline	12	.30	1	5	12	30	1	5
	bench	10	35	1	6	10	35	1	6
	press	8	40	1	7	8	40	1	7
		6	45	1	8	6	45	1	8
High Point		12	40	0	9	12	40	0	9
	flyes	12	30	2	10	12	30	2	9
Shoulders	military	12	15	1	5	12	15	1	5
	presses	10	20	1	6	10	20	1	6
		8	25	1	7	8	25	1	7
		6	30	1	8	6	30	1	8
High Point		12	25	0	9	12	25	0	9
	deltoid raise	12	10	2	10	12	10	2	9
Back	rows	12	30	1	5	12	30	1	5
	dumbbell	10	.35	1	6	10	35	1	6
		8	40	1	7	8	40	1	7
		6	45	1	8	6	45	1	8
High Point		12	40	0	9	12	40	1	9
	shrugs	12	40	2	10	12	40	1	9
Triceps	extensions	12	25	1	5	12	25	1	5
		10	30	1	6	12		48	6
		8	40	1	7	12		30	7
		6	50	1	8	12		30	8
High Point		12	40	0	9	12			9
	dips	12	12	2	10	12	2 actual		9

At this point, you should be 37 minutes into your upper body workout and have 9 minutes to go.

Biceps	curls	12	15	1	5	12	15	1	5
		10	20	1	6	10	20	1	6
		8	25	1	7	8	25		9
		6	30	1	8	6	30 +25	1	8
High Point		12	25	0	9	12	20		8
	hammer curl	12	20	–	10	12	25-20		8

Notes: _____ fly @ 30 – ? BP – 45

shrug – 40 30 lb

trice – dips – ??? – hammer C

Bill Phillips | Lesson-*for*-LIFE

"See where you're going before you get there."

Now that you've taken your before photo and are clear about where you're starting from, it's vitally important to develop an image or vision of where you want to go. One of the ways you can do that is to find an example, possibly one of the success stories in this book, of someone who's made the type of transformation you'd like to make. Try cutting out pictures of people whose transformation you admire and post them in some place where you can see them every day. Remember, the fact that they have succeeded is proof you can do it too! Focus on how good you will feel in that new, healthy, energetic body. The more you visualize your best body, the more empowered your mind-set will become, and the more resolve you will have to get there. Imagine it day and night, and let this fuel your success!

Success Story | Victor Carter

Age 41•Memphis, TN•Tennis Pro
Decreased Bodyfat from 28% to 14%

My before and after pictures clearly show the change in my physical appearance. However, I learned that it's not just what other people see that made this Program such a great success for me; it's what I see in myself. I see a new Vic Carter—a man with a renewed sense of purpose, happiness, and direction. I see a better example of smart, healthy living. And I also clearly see that Body-*for*-LIFE is about transforming your self-image, not just your body. It's about feeling like a winner and a Champion, not just looking like one.

DAY 2

Body-*for*-LIFE The Power Mindset

Please write down 5 things you can do between now and this time tomorrow
that will help you move forward in the direction of your 12-week goals.

	PLAN	ACTUAL
1	get up early - sleep well	
2	to the exercise	
3		
4		
5		

Body-*for*-LIFE The Universal Law of Reciprocation

Please write down 2 things you can do between now and
this time tomorrow to support and encourage others.

	PLAN	ACTUAL
1		
2		

Body-*for*-LIFE Focus on Progress, Not Perfection

Please write down 3 things you did very well today that helped
you move toward the achievement of your 12-week goals.

1	
2	
3	

Please write down one thing you will do even better tomorrow.

1	

Notes:

DAY 2

Body-*for*-LIFE The Eating-*for*-LIFE Method™

PLAN		ACTUAL	

Meal 1
PLAN — ☑ a.m. ☐ p.m. — 8:00 — protin-shak / apple

ACTUAL — ☐ a.m. ☐ p.m. — protn snake + (yptt) ⊘

Meal 2
PLAN — ☐ a.m. ☐ p.m. — 10:30 — myoplex

ACTUAL — ☐ a.m. ☐ p.m.

Meal 3
PLAN — ☐ a.m. ☐ p.m. — 1:00 — tuns

ACTUAL — ☐ a.m. ☐ p.m. — tuna

Meal 4
PLAN — ☐ a.m. ☐ p.m. — 4 — tuna

ACTUAL — ☐ a.m. ☐ p.m. — tuna

Meal 5
PLAN — ☐ a.m. ☐ p.m. — 7 — triuplx ($\frac{1}{2}$ Dc)

ACTUAL — ☐ a.m. ☑ p.m. — 7:0 — truplc

Meal 6
PLAN — ☐ a.m. ☐ p.m. — 10 — — chcah

ACTUAL — ☐ a.m. ☐ p.m. — myoplex

Notes: phen-free
phosphass   town 2

Body-*for*-LIFE | The 20-Minute Aerobics Solution™

Intensity Pattern

	PLAN		ACTUAL	
Planned Start Time: 7:05			Actual Start Time: 7:20	
Planned End Time: 7:25			Actual End Time: 7:41	
Time to Complete: 20 Minutes			Time to Complete: 21"	

Exercise	Minute by Minute	Intensity Level	Minute by Minute	Intensity Level
	1	5	1	5
	2	5	2	6
	3	6	3	7
P3	4	7	4	8
	5	8	5	8
20'	6	9	6	8
recumben	7	6	7	6
	8	7	8	7
	9	8	9	8
	10	9	10	9
	11	6	11	6
	12	7	12	7
	13	8	13	8
	14	9	14	9
	15	6	15	6
	16	7	16	7
	17	8	17	8
High Point	18	9	18	9
	19	10	19	9
	20	5	20	5

Notes: HR —max 183
— did not surpass
prev. C HR HR
tan (190)— if pul.HR

Bill Phillips — Lesson-*for*-LIFE

> "Life gives you the choice... either learn to overcome challenges or succumb to them."

One of the most important lessons I've learned is that life has numerous challenges in store for each of us, some expected, some unexpected. Some are merely "speed bumps," and others are like a brick wall. I've also learned that the mindset you use (or decide not to use) to face your life's challenges has a powerful impact on your experience of life, the development of your character and courage, as well as your self-image and self-esteem. Through the process of completing the 12-week Body-*for*-LIFE Program, you'll learn invaluable skills and undergo a great deal of training that will help you not only face but *overcome* your life's challenges! Literally and metaphorically, through Body-*for*-LIFE, you will learn to overcome resistance, improve your ability to creatively solve problems, and discover courage and character which, like a muscle, become stronger through proper training.

Success Story — Susan Maxey

Age 44 • Conyers, GA • Jewelry Designer/Artist
Decreased Bodyfat from 31% to 15%

A shell of my former self, I was going through a divorce after several unhappy years. I became a recluse, my health was bad, my eating and drinking were out of control, and I didn't care... I was totally self-destructing. My sister and best friend, who were very concerned, told me that they were entering the three of us in the Body-*for*-LIFE Challenge. This was just the spark I needed. At first, my commitment was half-hearted. But the longer I stuck with it, the better I felt! My confidence began to rise, which fueled my drive to succeed.

Body-*for*-LIFE   The Power Mindset

Please write down 5 things you can do between now and this time tomorrow that will help you move forward in the direction of your 12-week goals.

	PLAN	ACTUAL
1		
2		
3		
4		
5		

Body-*for*-LIFE   The Universal Law of Reciprocation

Please write down 2 things you can do between now and this time tomorrow to support and encourage others.

	PLAN	ACTUAL
1		
2		

Body-*for*-LIFE   Focus on Progress, Not Perfection

Please write down 3 things you did very well today that helped you move toward the achievement of your 12-week goals.

1	
2	
3	

Please write down one thing you will do even better tomorrow.

1	

Notes:

Body-*for*-LIFE   The Eating-*for*-LIFE Method™

PLAN	ACTUAL

Meal 1

☑ a.m.   Gulf phen-fr x(2)
☐ p.m.   (snak)
     T (apple)

Meal 1
☐ a.m.
☐ p.m.

Meal 2

☐ a.m.
☐ p.m.

Meal 2
☐ a.m.
☐ p.m.

Meal 3

☐ a.m.   sundwin
☐ p.m.   tuna

Meal 3
☐ a.m.
☐ p.m.

Meal 4

☐ a.m.
☐ p.m.

Meal 4
☐ a.m.
☐ p.m.

Meal 5   SASSAFRAS

☑ a.m.   or
☐ p.m.   SPCENDINS

Meal 5
☐ a.m.
☐ p.m.

Meal 6

☐ a.m.   - potn
☐ p.m.   snak

Meal 6
☐ a.m.
☐ p.m.

Notes:

DAY 3

Body-for-LIFE — Lower Body Workout

Intensity Pattern

	PLAN				ACTUAL			
Planned Start Time: 7:05					Actual Start Time: 7:55			
Planned End Time: 8:47					Actual End Time: 8:30			
Time to Complete: 42 Minutes					Time to Complete: 39"			

Lower Body Muscle Groups	Exercise	Reps	Weight (lbs)	Minutes Between Sets	Intensity Level	Reps	Weight (lbs)	Minutes Between Sets	Intensity Level
Quads	2x7	12	115	1	5	12	115	1	6
		10	120	1	6	10	120	1	7
		8	125	1	7	8	121	1	7
		6	125	1	8	6	125	1	8
High Point	2x7 squat	12	125	0	9	12	125	0	9
		12	90	2	10	12	30	2	9
Ham-strings	curls	12	45	1	5	12	45	1	5
		10	50	1	6	10	50	1	6
		8	55	1	7	8	55	1	7
		6	60	1	8	6	60	1	8
High Point	lunge	12	55	0	9	12	55	0	9
		12	35	2	10	12	35	2	10
Calves	2x7	12	35	1	5	12	35	1	8
		10	40	1	6	10	40	1	8
		8	45	1	7	8	45	1	8
		6	45	1	8	6	45		8
High Point	unilo	12	45	0	9	12	45	0	9
		12	25	2	10	12	25	2	8

At this point, you should be 31 minutes into your lower body workout and have 11 minutes to go.

Abs	reverse crunch	12	12	1	5	15	0		5
		10	10	1	6	10			6
		8	8	1	7	8			7
		6	6	1	8	8			8
High Point	ball	12	12	0	9	12			8
		12	12	-	10	12			8

Notes:

Bill Phillips — Lesson-*for*-LIFE

"You will change how you see, not just how you look."

I've witnessed transformations that surprise even me! And, having had the opportunity to meet many of these people, to talk with them, and learn from them, I've discovered that they didn't just change how they looked, they changed how they *see*. They view themselves, the people around them, and the world, in a new light.

Success Story — Carolyn Culverhouse

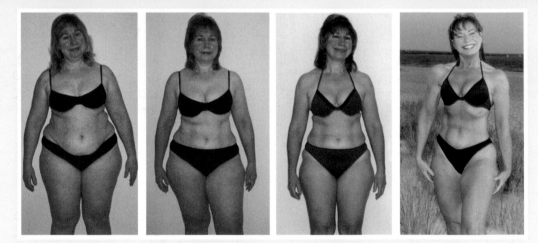

Age 51; Wilmington, NC; Registered Nurse
Completed Three 12-Week Challenges, Lost a Total of 80 lbs of Fat,
Lost 16 Inches Around the Hips; Transformed from a Size 20 Wardrobe to a Size 4

When I first began Body-*for*-LIFE, it was like standing at the bottom of the tallest mountain you could climb and looking up at a peak that was very nearly out of sight. I knew the journey could only be successful if I took it one step at a time. For me, the key was changing my thinking habits. I had to think like a healthy person in order to act like one. I had to think I was worth taking care of. I had to think I could do it. It took me 36 weeks, but I did it! I reached the top, and I feel better than I have ever felt in my whole life! Now I'm helping as many people as I can reach the top of the mountain they need to climb. I tell them, "You can do it!" And, "The view up here is amazing!"

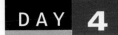

Body-*for*-LIFE The Power Mindset

Please write down 5 things you can do between now and this time tomorrow that will help you move forward in the direction of your 12-week goals.

	PLAN	ACTUAL
1		
2		
3		
4		
5		

Body-*for*-LIFE The Universal Law of Reciprocation

Please write down 2 things you can do between now and this time tomorrow to support and encourage others.

	PLAN	ACTUAL
1		
2		

Body-*for*-LIFE Focus on Progress, Not Perfection

Please write down 3 things you did very well today that helped you move toward the achievement of your 12-week goals.

1	
2	
3	

Please write down one thing you will do even better tomorrow.

1	

Notes:

DAY 4

Body-*for*-LIFE — The Eating-*for*-LIFE Method™

PLAN		ACTUAL	
Meal 1		**Meal 1**	
7 ☑ a.m. ☐ p.m.	*pnɔ̃ / ʃɾᴧ 1 ʿɪ̃*	☑ a.m. ☐ p.m.	*myup̃i*
Meal 2		**Meal 2**	
10 ☐ a.m. ☐ p.m.	*myupʃʎɾ*	☐ a.m. ☐ p.m.	*myupʃ*
Meal 3		**Meal 3**	
1 ☐ a.m. ☐ p.m.	*tᴧᵴ / ᴛ̶ᴏ̶p̶ʎ̶ᴛ̶ / ½*	☐ a.m. ☐ p.m.	*Tᴏᴘʎɾ / ½*
Meal 4		**Meal 4**	
4 ☐ a.m. ☐ p.m.	*tᴧᴠpʎᴧ ½*	☐ a.m. ☐ p.m.	*cᴘpᴧ / ᴛ ½ ᴛ·ᴛᴛ*
Meal 5		**Meal 5**	
7 ☐ a.m. ☐ p.m.	*7ᴧᴠpʎᴧ ½*	☐ a.m. ☐ p.m.	
Meal 6		**Meal 6**	
10 ☐ a.m. ☐ p.m.	*cᴧᴧᴧ / ᴛ ᴨ*	☐ a.m. ☐ p.m.	*TᴜᴛNᴄɪ / sᴛᴧᴧᴧᴠ*

Notes: *pᴧᴧ̃ᴧ−tᴧ ᴧ2*

Body-for-LIFE

The 20-Minute Aerobics Solution™

Intensity Pattern

	PLAN		ACTUAL	
	Planned Start Time: _____		Actual Start Time: _____	
	Planned End Time: _____		Actual End Time: _____	
	Time to Complete: 20 Minutes		Time to Complete: _____	
Exercise	Minute by Minute	Intensity Level	Minute by Minute	Intensity Level
	1	5	1	5
	2	5	2	6
recumbₐ	3	6	3	7
diceup	4	7	4	8
p3	5	8	5	3
p∩J∩	6	9	6	5
	7	6	7	6
	8	7	8	7
	9	8	9	8
	10	9	10	9
	11	6	11	5
	12	7	12	7
	13	8	13	7
	14	9	14	8
	15	6	15	5
	16	7	16	6
	17	8	17	7
High Point	18	9	18	8
	19	10	19	9
	20	5	20	9

Notes: gₐ∩ vₑ 7. un7 （160）—

ᵒᵁᴅvₚᵣ.1 —2l7ₐ7 1 mₑₐᵤ

ₑvₑ7 ₑ7h7

296 cul

Bill Phillips | Lesson-*for*-LIFE

"You must give each and every workout your best effort, and then some!"

One of the most important lessons I have to share is that each and every workout you perform matters. You've got just 12 weeks to achieve the goals you've set. That's just 18 upper body workouts, 18 lower body workouts, and 36 aerobic sessions. You must give each and every workout your best effort, *and then some!* One of the best ways to boost workout intensity is by increasing your ability to harness your mental power. You can do that by focusing your mind while you carefully plan your workouts ahead of time. Then, imagine going through your workout. Rehearse it. *See* yourself hitting your high points *before* you even step into the gym. *See* yourself succeeding. Starting with today's upper body workout, go to the next level of training intensity! Test your inner strength today and make this workout count!

Success Story | Rory Palazzo

Age 29 • Highlands Ranch, CO • Business Analyst
Gained 9 lbs of Muscle, Lost 21 lbs of Fat

I was genuinely unhappy with the way I looked. I realized that I needed to take control of my life. Once I had set goals and burned positive patterns into my routine, it was not difficult to stay on track. I reviewed my goals and looked at inspiring images every night and every morning before I worked out. I envisioned how good I would feel (and look) when I reached my goals. That vision and desire inspired me to stay on course. I believe in myself now more than ever before. I feel as if my whole life has been empowered.

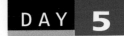

Body-*for*-LIFE The Power Mindset

Please write down 5 things you can do between now and this time tomorrow
that will help you move forward in the direction of your 12-week goals.

	PLAN	ACTUAL
1		
2		
3		
4		
5		

Body-*for*-LIFE The Universal Law of Reciprocation

Please write down 2 things you can do between now and
this time tomorrow to support and encourage others.

	PLAN	ACTUAL
1		
2		

Body-*for*-LIFE Focus on Progress, Not Perfection

Please write down 3 things you did very well today that helped
you move toward the achievement of your 12-week goals.

1	
2	
3	

Please write down one thing you will do even better tomorrow.

1	

Notes:

Body-*for*-LIFE The Eating-*for*-LIFE Method™

PLAN	ACTUAL

Meal 1

- [x] a.m.
- [ ] p.m.

8:00

pNTln
rnch.
T cp.t

Meal 1

- [ ] a.m.
- [ ] p.m.

Meal 2

- [x] a.m.
- [ ] p.m.

10:3.

my.1

Meal 2

- [ ] a.m.
- [ ] p.m.

Meal 3

- [ ] a.m.
- [x] p.m.

1

1ʋʋ1ʌ
—f..ʌ
T
r.lʌl

Meal 3

- [ ] a.m.
- [ ] p.m.

Meal 4

- [ ] a.m.
- [x] p.m.

4

B ar

Meal 4

- [ ] a.m.
- [ ] p.m.

Meal 5

- [ ] a.m.
- [ ] p.m.

7

chum
+
rcl.u

Meal 5

- [ ] a.m.
- [ ] p.m.

Meal 6

- [ ] a.m.
- [ ] p.m.

10

p~r.

Meal 6

- [ ] a.m.
- [ ] p.m.

Notes: ⌐ 173.7 l

Body-*for*-LIFE Upper Body Workout

Intensity Pattern

	PLAN	ACTUAL
Planned Start Time: 6:05		Actual Start Time: _____
Planned End Time: 6:51		Actual End Time: _____
Time to Complete: 46 Minutes		Time to Complete: 46-40

Upper Body Muscle Groups	Exercise	Reps	Weight (lbs)	Minutes Between Sets	Intensity Level	Reps	Weight (lbs)	Minutes Between Sets	Intensity Level
Chest	inclin	12	35	1	5	12	35	1	5
	press	10	40	1	6	10	40	1	6
		8	45	1	7 2:34	8	45	1	7
		6	45	1	8 4:15	6	45	1	8
High Point	f m.	12	45	0	9 5:55	12	45 44:0	0	9
		12	30	2	10	12	30	2	9
Shoulders	prss	12	20	1	5	12	20	1	5
		10	25	1	6	10 9	25	1	6 (7)
		8	30	1	7	8 7	30	1	7 (8)
		6	35	1	8 15	6 6)	35	1	8 (9)
High Point	la ram	12	30	0	9 16:15	12	35 30/25/35 3 2 20		9
		12	10	2	10	12	10	2	9
Back	f lw	12	35	1	5 20:15	12	35	1	6
		10	40	1	6 22:20	10	40	1	7
		8	45	1	7 23:4	8	48	1	8
		6	45	1	8 25:3	6	46	1	9
High Point	shr	12	45	0	9	12	48	0	
		12	30	2	10 27	12	46	2	
Triceps	ext	12	25	1	5 30:05	12	25	1	7
		10		1	6	10	45		8
		8		1	7	8	30		8
		6		1	8	6	15		8
High Point	dip	12	25	0	9	12	25		8
		12	0	2	10	12 4+0FNR			8

At this point, you should be 37 minutes into your upper body workout and have 9 minutes to go.

Biceps	curls	12	20	1	5	12	20	1	6
		10	25	1	6	10	25	1	7
		8	30	1	7	8	30 27	1	8
		6	35	1	8	6	35	1	9
High Point		12	30	0	9 45	12	20	0	8
		12	25	–	10	12	45	2	9

Notes:
_____
_____

Bill Phillips — Lesson-*for*-LIFE

"A little 'extra nothing' can go a long way."

The pursuit of worthy goals requires hard work, persistence, and intense focus. There's no doubt about it. However, one of the important lessons I've learned over the years is that sometimes a little "extra nothing" can go a long way. By that I mean don't underestimate the importance of rest and relaxation. A certain amount of "down time," or free time, helps renew energy, clear the mind, and heal the body. That's why one day out of every seven, on the Body-*for*-LIFE Program, I encourage you to take a break. Eat whatever you want, don't exercise, don't plan, don't record anything in your journal. Just flat out take the day off from anything Body-*for*-LIFE-related. And certainly don't feel guilty about doing some extra nothing. It's part of the process of making progress and succeeding. So enjoy tomorrow, your first free day—you've earned it!☺

Success Story — Carolyn Pagnato

Age 35 • Vienna, VA • Mother
Gained Energy, Lost 14 lbs of Fat
Decreased Bodyfat from 21% to 17%

My before and after photos show how my body has changed, but what really excites me most is my smile! That's the reflection of how I really feel! I have become more content, more disciplined, and more confident. And I've learned to love the *process* of becoming fit: preparing healthy meals, planning and recording my workouts, and relaxing on my free day. I've also discovered that success is in the everyday accomplishments needed to achieve extraordinary results over time. What day counts? Today and every day!!!

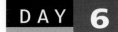

DAY 6

Body-*for*-LIFE   The Power Mindset

Please write down 5 things you can do between now and this time tomorrow
that will help you move forward in the direction of your 12-week goals.

	PLAN	ACTUAL
1		
2		
3		
4		
5		

Body-*for*-LIFE   The Universal Law of Reciprocation

Please write down 2 things you can do between now and
this time tomorrow to support and encourage others.

	PLAN	ACTUAL
1		
2		

Body-*for*-LIFE   Focus on Progress, Not Perfection

Please write down 3 things you did very well today that helped
you move toward the achievement of your 12-week goals.

1	
2	
3	

Please write down one thing you will do even better tomorrow.

1	

Notes:

Body-*for*-LIFE The Eating-*for*-LIFE Method™

PLAN			ACTUAL		
Meal 1			**Meal 1**		
8	☑ a.m. ☐ p.m.	?:00 protein shake + protein	9:10	☑ a.m. ☐ p.m.	myoplex pro
Meal 2			**Meal 2**		
10:30	☐ a.m. ☐ p.m.	myoplex shake	12:30	☑ a.m. ☐ p.m.	myoplex pro
Meal 3			**Meal 3**		
1:00	☐ a.m. ☐ p.m.	~~reg.~~ tuna sandwich	2:30	☐ a.m. ☐ p.m.	
Meal 4			**Meal 4**		
4:00	☐ a.m. ☐ p.m.	myoplex	5:30	☐ a.m. ☐ p.m.	Myoplex pro
Meal 5			**Meal 5**		
7:00	☐ a.m. ☐ p.m.	chick	8:08	☐ a.m. ☐ p.m.	tuna
Meal 6			**Meal 6**		
10:00	☐ a.m. ☐ p.m.	myoplex tun	10:00	☐ a.m. ☐ p.m.	Myoplex shake

Notes: 173.5 lb

2 pren-free

myoplex ?? @ 9:1?

Body-*for*-LIFE

The 20-Minute Aerobics Solution™

Intensity Pattern

	PLAN		ACTUAL	
Planned Start Time: 7:00			Actual Start Time: 8:00	
Planned End Time: 7:20			Actual End Time: 8:20	
Time to Complete: 20 Minutes			Time to Complete: 20"	
Exercise	Minute by Minute	Intensity Level	Minute by Minute	Intensity Level
P3	1	5	1	5
	2	5	2	6
	3	6	3	7
	4	7	4	8
	5	8	5	9
	6	9	6	5
	7	6	7	6
	8	7	8	7
	9	8	9	8
	10	9	10	9
	11	6	11	5
	12	7	12	6
	13	8	13	7
	14	9	14	8
	15	6	15	6
	16	7	16	7
	17	8	17	8
High Point	18	9	18	9
	19	10	19	9
	20	5	20	5

Notes: 5.55 m
(172 BPM)
under to
put on (180)

Bill Phillips — Lesson-*for*-LIFE

> "The last thing you want to do is often the first thing you need to do!"

I've talked to thousands and thousands of people who have completed the Body-*for*-LIFE Program and achieved extraordinary results, and not a single one has said anything remotely akin to, "Bill, I just couldn't wait to take that before photo!" Or, "Bill, I love dragging my butt out of bed at 5:00 A.M., putting on my workout clothes, and doing an intense workout!" I know how it is because I feel the same way. However, it's vitally important to recognize that the feeling of not wanting to do something is actually an opportunity to exercise your inner strength. You see, when the last thing you want to do is get out of bed early in the morning and work out intensely, but you do it anyway, you immediately experience a burst of positive energy. And the more you exercise your self-discipline in this way, the stronger, healthier, and more energetic you'll become!

Success Story — Julie Moss

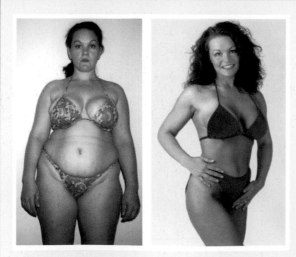

Age 31•Baltimore, MD• Mother of 5
Gained Strength and Energy, Lost 46 lbs of Fat
Reduced Bodyfat from 30% to 15%

I was desperately searching for inspiration to get my figure back and wear a pair of jeans again. I had just been pregnant for 18 months. My fifth child, Gabrielle, was born in July 1999, 10 months after her sister Haley. Raising five children is definitely an obstacle when it comes to finding time to work out, but I was able to make time where I thought there was none. Even if it meant working out at 5:00 in the morning after feeding the baby, I found that overcoming adversities enabled me to stand proud and say I did it!

Body-*for*-LIFE The Power Mindset

Please write down 5 things you can do between now and this time tomorrow
that will help you move forward in the direction of your 12-week goals.

	PLAN	ACTUAL
1	- drink 10 glass of wate.	
	- eat 6 nutrition meals	
2	- GNC - 2 protein shake	
	myoplx	
3		
4		
5		

Body-*for*-LIFE The Universal Law of Reciprocation

Please write down 2 things you can do between now and
this time tomorrow to support and encourage others.

	PLAN	ACTUAL
1		
2		

Body-*for*-LIFE Focus on Progress, Not Perfection

Please write down 3 things you did very well today that helped
you move toward the achievement of your 12-week goals.

1	- completed run for later
2	
3	

Please write down one thing you will do even better tomorrow.

1	

Notes:

DAY 8

Body-*for*-LIFE   The Eating-*for*-LIFE Method™

PLAN	ACTUAL

Meal 1

PLAN	ACTUAL
☑ a.m. ☐ p.m.	☐ a.m. ☐ p.m.
9:30 am	protein - bar
phospher HP	serous
- protin shok	

Meal 2

PLAN	ACTUAL
☐ a.m. ☐ p.m.	☐ a.m. ☑ p.m.
	myopla
	snak - ren, ll
	12:30 m

Meal 3

PLAN	ACTUAL
☐ a.m. ☐ p.m.	☐ a.m. ☐ p.m.
	chicken - salca
	scnauur

Meal 4

PLAN	ACTUAL
☐ a.m. ☐ p.m.	☐ a.m. ☐ p.m.

Meal 5

PLAN	ACTUAL
☐ a.m. ☐ p.m.	☐ a.m. ☑ p.m. 7:66
	myopla
	snak - R70

Meal 6

PLAN	ACTUAL
☐ a.m. ☐ p.m.	☐ a.m. ☑ p.m. 9:30
	- Trioplex
	pecnun bone
	cnc try

Notes: ___ 178.510 - upn auu

Body-*for*-LIFE — Lower Body Workout

Intensity Pattern

	PLAN	ACTUAL
Planned Start Time: 8:30		Actual Start Time: 8:30
Planned End Time: 9:12		Actual End Time:
Time to Complete: 42 Minutes		Time to Complete: 39.18

Lower Body Muscle Groups	Exercise	Reps	Weight (lbs)	Minutes Between Sets	Intensity Level	Reps	Weight (lbs)	Minutes Between Sets	Intensity Level
Quads	2 x 7	12	100	1	5		✓	1	5
		10	110	1	6		✓	1	6
	↓	8	120	1	7		✓	1	7
		6	125	1	8		✓	1	8
High Point	squat	12	120	0	9			1	9
		12	90	2	10			1	8
Hamstrings	curls	12	35	1	5	12	35	1	4
		10	40	1	6	10	40	1	5
		8	45	1	7	8	45	1	7
	↓	6	50	1	8	6	50	1	8
High Point	lunges	12	45	0	9	12	45	1	9
		12	25	2	10	12	25	1	9
Calves	extensn'	12	25	1	5	12	25	1	5
		10	30	1	6	10	30		6
		8	35	1	7	8	35	↓	7
		6	40	1	8	6	40		7
High Point		12	35	0	9	12	40		8
		12	25	2	10				8

At this point, you should be 31 minutes into your lower body workout and have 11 minutes to go.

		Reps	Weight (lbs)	Minutes Between Sets	Intensity Level	Reps	Weight (lbs)	Minutes Between Sets	Intensity Level
Abs	reverse crun~	12	12	1	5	12	—	45'	5
		10	10	1	6	10	—		6
		8	8	1	7	8	—		7
		6	6	1	8	6	—	✓	8
High Point	sit~can~	12		0	9				8
		12		—	10	12			8

Notes: Ø high point.
1 by side — quadr ext ⎫
            — ₁₂ curls ⎬ next wk
            — calvs   ⎭

Bill Phillips — Lesson-*for*-LIFE

"You have the power to change, and no one can take that away!"

Imagine, less than 11 weeks from now, having the energy to go all-out from dawn to dusk, having the confidence to do things you've been putting off, having the certainty to make the right decision at the right time, knowing you can regain control over virtually anything in this world if you set your mind to it. Well, you will! And it doesn't matter if you're 22 or 62, man or woman, fit or unfit. No matter who you are, this much I promise: You have the power to change! Please read the success stories in this book and you will see. These people emerged from those 12 weeks with a healthier body and a new, exciting life. They are the proof—the living, breathing, walking, talking proof—that the Body-*for*-LIFE Program can help you change your life, too. The process of creating *your* new Body-*for*-LIFE has already begun. Keep up the good work!

Success Story — Porter Freeman

Age 53 • Golden, CO • BFL Spokesperson
Gained Energy, Lost 54 lbs of Fat

Anyone can do what I, and thousands of others who have followed the Body-*for*-LIFE Program, have done. Don't let anybody tell you that you can't do it. You *can.* It's up to you. Decide to do it, and then follow through. I'm telling you, if a 260-lb old-timer can do it, anyone can do it! I talk with people every day who want to look and feel better. I tell them they can feel as good as I feel. They can make that U-turn. Everyone can change! I plan to spend the rest of my life helping people get healthy.

Body-*for*-LIFE The Power Mindset

Please write down 5 things you can do between now and this time tomorrow that will help you move forward in the direction of your 12-week goals.

	PLAN	ACTUAL
1	_wake up early & do cardio-_ _20" - HIIT - recumb in b.._	
2	_eat 6 nutritious meals_	
3	_plan more appoint-ment - less_ _engineered food - got Neuin fruits_	
4		
5		

Body-*for*-LIFE The Universal Law of Reciprocation

Please write down 2 things you can do between now and this time tomorrow to support and encourage others.

	PLAN	ACTUAL
1	_encourage program to 2 others_	
2		

Body-*for*-LIFE Focus on Progress, Not Perfection

Please write down 3 things you did very well today that helped you move toward the achievement of your 12-week goals.

1	
2	
3	

Please write down one thing you will do even better tomorrow.

1	

Notes:

DAY 9

Body-*for*-LIFE — The Eating-*for*-LIFE Method™

PLAN		ACTUAL	

Meal 1

8:30 — ☑ a.m. ☐ p.m.
protein-shake
+ myoplex x ②
+ apple

8:30 — ☑ a.m. ☐ p.m.
।
ऽ
apple

Meal 2

11:00 — ☐ a.m. ☐ p.m.
myoplex

11:00 — ☑ a.m. ☐ p.m.
myoplex

Meal 3

2:00 — ☐ a.m. ☐ p.m.
~~eaten~~
tuna salad

☐ a.m. ☐ p.m.
chicken
salad

Meal 4

☑ a.m. ☐ p.m.
myoplex

☐ a.m. ☐ p.m.
myoplex

Meal 5

☐ a.m. ☐ p.m.

☐ a.m. ☐ p.m.

Meal 6

16 — ☑ a.m. ☐ p.m.
2 protein
+ ...
11:00

11 — ☐ a.m. ☑ p.m.
protein
+ green pea
- small piece of ...
+ 2 slices of ...

Notes: 2 protein-free capsun + 2 slices + 7 ...

Body-for-LIFE

The 20-Minute Aerobics Solution™

Intensity Pattern	PLAN		ACTUAL	
	Planned Start Time: 7:20		Actual Start Time: 7:20	
	Planned End Time: 7:40		Actual End Time: 7:40	
	Time to Complete: 20 Minutes		Time to Complete: 21 m	

Exercise	Minute by Minute	Intensity Level	Minute by Minute	Intensity Level
recumbent bicycle P3 — level 3	1	5	1	5
	2	5	2	6
	3	6	3	7
	4	7	4	8
	5	8	5	8
	6	9	6	9
	7	6	7	6
	8	7	8	8
	9	8	9	8
	10	9	10	9
	11	6	11	6
	12	7	12	7
	13	8	13	8
	14	9	14	9
	15	6	15	6
	16	7	16	7
	17	8	17	8
High Point	18	9	18	8
	19	10	19	9
2'	20	5	20	9

Notes:
- distance 5.25
  co 325
- HR went up to (187)
  went down 7 (149) — time 21
  RCA in 120 - 2c

Bill Phillips　　Lesson-*for*-LIFE

"The most important person to stand up to is yourself."

Sometimes you may feel as if you're having a tug of war between your old self and your new self. It's not easy to make the type of changes in your life that you've decided to make. In your moments of decision, when you feel like eating ice cream at night or lying in bed in the morning instead of getting up to work out, ask yourself, "Who do I want to be today: the old me or the new me?" Your body and life are being shaped by these moment-to-moment decisions. It's those decisions that brought you to where you were at the beginning of this Program. And if you continue to make decisions the old way, you're going to continue to produce the same results. To create different results, you have to take a different approach. It's not easy to stand up to yourself, but you can do it!

Success Story　　Donna Szabo

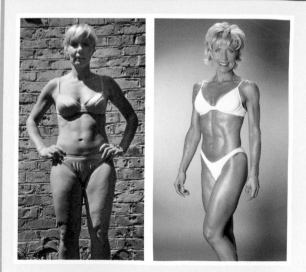

Age 41 • Raleigh, NC • Decorative Painter/Mother
Decreased Bodyfat from 19% to 12%

My motivation to change was sparked when I was shopping for a swimsuit to hide my fat and I realized I needed a wetsuit! I was unhappy. After I completed the Challenge, what I once saw as an obstacle was really only an excuse. I was the obstacle. Fear and self-doubt had turned me into a procrastinator. How could I fail at something I never began? Once I grabbed the bull by the horns, faced my fears, and accepted responsibility for my actions, I turned my excuses into reasons for completing the Challenge.

Body-*for*-LIFE The Power Mindset

Please write down 5 things you can do between now and this time tomorrow that will help you move forward in the direction of your 12-week goals.

	PLAN	ACTUAL
1	[illegible]	
2	- take care (?) of my teeth (?)	
3	- restaurant (?) - be rigid + discipline (?)	
4		
5		

Body-*for*-LIFE The Universal Law of Reciprocation

Please write down 2 things you can do between now and this time tomorrow to support and encourage others.

	PLAN	ACTUAL
1		
2		

Body-*for*-LIFE Focus on Progress, Not Perfection

Please write down 3 things you did very well today that helped you move toward the achievement of your 12-week goals.

1 - [illegible] with [illegible] - completing (?) [illegible] - [illegible] of work
2 - completed my exam (?) [illegible]
3

Please write down one thing you will do even better tomorrow.

1 exciting (?) about (?) tomorrow (?)

Notes:

Body-for-LIFE   The Eating-for-LIFE Method™

PLAN		ACTUAL	

Meal 1

☑ a.m.	פרוטין	☐ a.m.	פרוטין shake
☐ p.m.	shake	☐ p.m.	+
	apple		apple

Meal 2

| ☐ a.m. | myoplex | ☐ a.m. | |
| ☐ p.m. | | ☐ p.m. | |

Meal 3

| ☐ a.m. | | ☐ a.m. | |
| ☐ p.m. | | ☐ p.m. | |

Meal 4

	נוגריר		
☐ a.m.	בר	☐ a.m.	Sandwm
☐ p.m.		☐ p.m.	

Meal 5

	salan		fish (Bream)
☐ a.m.	+	☐ a.m.	+
☐ p.m.	fish	☐ p.m.	salla
			7 sugar

Meal 6

| ☐ a.m. | | ☐ a.m. | |
| ☐ p.m. | | ☐ p.m. | |

Notes: ___2 pm fr @ lin___
___dia pownt - unpapau___
___fr 3 meup___
___ari wajt e___
___the restua___

Body-*for*-LIFE — Upper Body Workout

Intensity Pattern

	PLAN		ACTUAL	
Planned Start Time: 6:05			Actual Start Time: 6:10	
Planned End Time: 6:51			Actual End Time: 7:00	
Time to Complete: 46 Minutes			Time to Complete: 56"	

Upper Body Muscle Groups	Exercise	Reps	Weight (lbs)	Minutes Between Sets	Intensity Level	Reps	Weight (lbs)	Minutes Between Sets	Intensity Level
Chest	inclin BP	12	30	1	5	12	30	1.9	5
	bench	10	35	1	6 1.9"	10	35	'	6-7
	press	8	40	1	7	8	40		7
		6	45	1	8	6	45		8
High Point		12	40	0	9	⑨12	40	0	3
		12	25	2	10	12	25	2	3
Shoulders	shulla	12	20	1	5 10:05	12	27	1	6
	prs-	10	25	1	6	10(8)	25	1	8
		8	30	1	7 new	8(6)	30	1	9
		6	35	1	8	4	35	1	3
High Point		12	30	0	9	12	30/25/20 2 4	0	8
	c 17 via, va	12	10	2	10	17(1)	10		9
Back	dumb-bill row	12	25	1	5 21 50	12	25	1"	5
		10	30	1	6	10	30	1'	6
		8	35	1	7	8	35	1'	6
		6	40	1	8	6	40		7
High Point		12	35	0	9		35		8
	bent rau	12	10	2	10		10		9
Triceps	dumbell ext	12	20	1	5	12	25	1"	12
		10	15	1	6	10		45	10
		8	20	1	7	8		30	8
		6	25	1	8	6		15	6
High Point		12		0	9	12		0	12
	ays	12		2	10	12			8

At this point, you should be 37 minutes into your upper body workout and have 9 minutes to go.

Biceps	curr	12	15	1	5	12	15	1	12
	dip-	10	20	1	6	10	20	1	10
	(b.1)	8	25	1	7	8	25	1	8
		6	30	1	8	6	30	1	6
High Point		12	25	0	9	12	20		8
	hammer	12	20	–	10	12	20		8

Notes: BP— ory cdr 7, ach.u 3/12 @ leul ⑨ inten,n -bp
shular prs - onpe rj 5 la -nu e is
dumpul nwr 9 hjs   onj finy nr
use E-Z Dur clnurmn w. - bench dr—
tewi,n—1nn or w

Bill Phillips — Lesson-*for*-LIFE

"Have faith in what you see."

I am often asked questions about the Program, such as: "Why do 20 minutes of aerobics instead of 15? Why not do 5 reps instead of 6 on your heaviest set? Why eat 6 meals a day instead of 5? Can a person like me succeed at this? Isn't it impossible to change so much so fast?" By far and away, the vast majority of these questions can be answered with just two words: "Have faith." Not blind faith; just the opposite. *Have faith in what you see!* The dozens of success stories you'll read about in this book represent literally hundreds of thousands of people who have achieved extraordinary results. And, by and large, they followed the Body-*for*-LIFE Program to the letter. The Program, as it's designed, works. That is a fact. I highly encourage you to have faith, not just in me, but in the other people who have successfully completed the Program. And, most important of all, *have faith in yourself.* You will succeed when you give yourself the opportunity. I promise.

Success Story — Robert and Darcy Custer

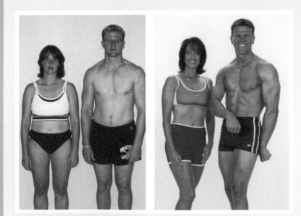

Ages 35 • Oklahoma City, OK
Minister and Homemaker
Robert Reduced Bodyfat from 14% to 6%
Darcy Reduced Bodyfat from 32% to 18%
Combined, Gained 14 lbs of Muscle, Lost 47 lbs of Fat

Our motivation began the moment we saw our before photos (oh, how humbling!). One of Bill's articles spoke of having faith and believing in the Program. Because we're ministers, his statement hit home. We meticulously applied his principles to our life by setting specific and measurable goals and then posting them on our refrigerator. Our passion inspired others to accept the Challenge. We feel great again. We even look forward to putting on our bathing suits. We put our heart and soul into this Challenge, and we did it together!

Body-*for*-LIFE   The Power Mindset

Please write down 5 things you can do between now and this time tomorrow
that will help you move forward in the direction of your 12-week goals.

	PLAN	ACTUAL
1	– get up @ 6:00–6:20 – for c++a- – pry tm @ (MEIDITSS)	
2		
3		
4		
5		

Body-*for*-LIFE   The Universal Law of Reciprocation

Please write down 2 things you can do between now and
this time tomorrow to support and encourage others.

	PLAN	ACTUAL
1	–	
2		

Body-*for*-LIFE   Focus on Progress, Not Perfection

Please write down 3 things you did very well today that helped
you move toward the achievement of your 12-week goals.

1	– less fear of failure
2	– well thgn planed-work, planning, relaxing
3	

Please write down one thing you will do even better tomorrow.

1	

Notes:

Body-*for*-LIFE The Eating-*for*-LIFE Method™

PLAN		ACTUAL	

Meal 1

PLAN:
- ☑ a.m. ☐ p.m. 7:30 ארוחת בוקר
- שומן
- ↑
- ph...ph...

ACTUAL:
- ☑ a.m. ☐ p.m. 9:30
- ארוחת בוקר (apple)
- שומן

Meal 2

PLAN:
- ☐ a.m. ☐ p.m. 10:00 – Trapit

ACTUAL:
- ☐ a.m. ☐ p.m. salmon
- ½ salad

Meal 3

PLAN:
- whole weal
- ☐ a.m. ☑ p.m. rice tuna
- ½

ACTUAL:
- ☐ a.m. ☐ p.m. swim
- ½ rm

Meal 4

PLAN:
- 3:30 ☑ a.m. ☑ p.m. 1. Tuna

ACTUAL:
- ☑ a.m. ☐ p.m. tuna

Meal 5

PLAN:
- myoplex
- 6:00 ☐ a.m. ☑ p.m.

ACTUAL:
- ☐ a.m. ☐ p.m. tuna

Meal 6

PLAN:
- ☐ a.m. ☑ p.m. 9:35 – med
- C
- mm
- ארוחת ערב

ACTUAL:
- ☐ a.m. ☐ p.m. hamburger
- ↑
- rice (wild)

Notes: _____ ארוחת—תא ... בריאה ... רא) _____

Body-*for*-LIFE

The 20-Minute Aerobics Solution™

Intensity Pattern

	PLAN		ACTUAL	
	Planned Start Time: 6:00		Actual Start Time: 6:20	
	Planned End Time: 6:20		Actual End Time: 6,41	
	Time to Complete: 20 Minutes		Time to Complete: 21	

Exercise	Minute by Minute	Intensity Level	Minute by Minute	Intensity Level
recumbent p.N (P3) level 3 20" T 1"	1	5	1	5
	2	5	2	6
	3	6	3	7
	4	7	4	8
	5	8	5	9
	6	9	6	9
	7	6	7	6
	8	7	8	7
	9	8	9	8
	10	9	10	9
	11	6	11	9
	12	7	12	6
	13	8	13	6
	14	9	14	7
	15	6	15	8
	16	7	16	7
	17	8	17	8
High Point	18	9	18	9
	19	10	19	10
	20	5	20	

Notes: HR up to 185 → 145 1"
5.30 Km
329 culvi-

Bill Phillips — Lesson-*for*-LIFE

"Invest your time, don't just spend it!"

Time, much more precious than money, is there for us to invest or squander. Each and every day, we are given the exact same amount of time to work with—1,440 minutes. Where you are in life and where you will go is largely determined by what you do with that time. Spend time carelessly and you will pay the price: poor health, frustration, low energy, depression. Invest your time wisely—by properly caring for your body, by exercising and eating right—and you will enjoy a healthy rate of return. Among the rewards are increased positive energy and clarity. Those paybacks allow you to do more in the time you have to work with. Today, please think about what you are doing with *your* time. Are you *investing* it wisely? Are you spending more time than you need to on things that are not productive, inspiring, or important to you? How can you improve?

Success Story — Pete Holter

Age 23 • Papillion, NE • Programmer, USAF
Gained 20 lbs of Muscle, Lost 11 lbs of Fat

I was distracted, bored, and discouraged. Then one day, I finally decided I'd had enough. No more excuses—it was time for a change. I realized that committing myself to this Program helped me eliminate indecisiveness. I used to waste so much time figuring out what I should do with myself that I often ended up doing nothing. Now I take charge in all areas of my life. I thought there was no way I had the time to devote to improving myself. But now I feel I have at least twice as much time and energy.

Body-*for*-LIFE The Power Mindset

Please write down 5 things you can do between now and this time tomorrow that will help you move forward in the direction of your 12-week goals.

	PLAN	ACTUAL
1	- protien call	
2	- wu-hut 6:00 -6:45 w legs	
	- eating 7 eat healthy	
3	stay focussing, stay organized	
4		
5		

Body-*for*-LIFE The Universal Law of Reciprocation

Please write down 2 things you can do between now and this time tomorrow to support and encourage others.

	PLAN	ACTUAL
1		
2		

Body-*for*-LIFE Focus on Progress, Not Perfection

Please write down 3 things you did very well today that helped you move toward the achievement of your 12-week goals.

1	
2	
3	

Please write down one thing you will do even better tomorrow.

1	

Notes:

DAY 12

Body-*for*-LIFE The Eating-*for*-LIFE Method™

PLAN		ACTUAL	
Meal 1		**Meal 1**	
☑ a.m. ☐ p.m.	7:00 protein shake + PHOSPHATES (apple)	☐ a.m. ☐ p.m.	
Meal 2		**Meal 2**	
☑ a.m. ☐ p.m.	Tropis (½)	☐ a.m. ☐ p.m.	
Meal 3		**Meal 3**	
1:00 ☐ a.m. ☐ p.m.	salmon rice	☐ a.m. ☐ p.m.	
Meal 4	Tropis (½)	**Meal 4**	
4:00 ☐ a.m. ☐ p.m.		☐ a.m. ☐ p.m.	
Meal 5	salad Fish/chicken	**Meal 5**	
☑ a.m. ☐ p.m.		☐ a.m. ☐ p.m.	
Meal 6		**Meal 6**	
☐ a.m. ☐ p.m.		☐ a.m. ☐ p.m.	

Notes: phosphocreatine
ptien-free 12 7:00

Body-*for*-LIFE — Lower Body Workout

Intensity Pattern

PLAN

Planned Start Time: 6:00
Planned End Time: 6:42
Time to Complete: 42 Minutes

ACTUAL

Actual Start Time: 6:20
Actual End Time: 7
Time to Complete: 41'37

Lower Body Muscle Groups	Exercise	Reps	Weight (lbs)	Minutes Between Sets	Intensity Level	Reps	Weight (lbs)	Minutes Between Sets	Intensity Level
Quads	2 x 7	12	110	1	5	12	110	1	5-6
		10	115	1	6	10	115	1	6-7
		8	120	1	7	8	120	1	8
		6	125	1	8	6	125	1	9
High Point	squat	12	125	0	9	12	125	0	9
		12	90	2	10	12	90	2	8
Hamstrings	curls	12	40	1	5	12	40	1	5
		10	45	1	6	10	45	1	6
		8	50	1	7	8	50	1	7
		6	55	1	8	6	55	1	
High Point	lunge	12	50	0	9	12	50	0	
		12	30	2	10	12	30	2	
Calves		12	30	1	5	12	30	1	5
		10	35	1	6	10	35	1	6
		8	40	1	7	8	40	1	7
		6	45	1	8	7	40	1	7
High Point	con.fir.	12	40	0	9	12	40	0	8
		12		2	10	12	25	2	9

At this point, you should be 31 minutes into your lower body workout and have 11 minutes to go.

Abs	reverse crunch	12	12	1	5	12	0	1	5
	ab do	10	10	1	6	10	5	1	6
		8	8	1	7	8	10	1	7
		6	6	1	8	6	15	1	8
High Point	ball	12		0	9	12	0		9
	reverse	12		–	10	12			8

Notes:

Bill Phillips　Lesson-*for*-LIFE

"When you make a change, you make a difference."

The Body-*for*-LIFE Program is designed to help you make a change, A change in the way you look; a change in the way you see. And when you make a change, *you make a difference*. And by that, I mean you become a positive example of what's possible. You become an inspiration to others. Please think about that today. When you do, I believe you'll find even more purpose, more meaning, and more passion to continue on. And you'll join the thousands of unsung heroes who have also made a change and are making a difference. They're moms, dads, students, teachers, business owners, Air Force fighter pilots, firefighters, secretaries, and surgeons. They are from *all* walks of life. These people are the driving force at the center of the evolving global Body-*for*-LIFE community. They're improving their outlook on life and helping others to do the same!

Success Story　Jerry Braam

**Age 38 • Springfield, MO • Respiratory Practitioner
Decreased Bodyfat from 30% to 10%
Gained Energy and Strength**

In my practice, I advise patients daily about the importance of health care, but I was living a contradiction because I was not caring for my own body the way I should have been. I didn't necessarily "want" to do the Body-*for*-LIFE Program, but I *needed* to. One day at a time, I completely rebuilt my body. People say I look years younger, and I've never felt better. As a result, I face each day with anticipation, and the new body I see in the mirror tells me I will succeed. Now that I'm centered, I'm able to give freely.

Body-*for*-LIFE   The Power Mindset

Please write down 5 things you can do between now and this time tomorrow
that will help you move forward in the direction of your 12-week goals.

	PLAN	ACTUAL
1	do the cycling 6 nutritious meals/a	
2		
3		
4		
5		

Body-*for*-LIFE   The Universal Law of Reciprocation

Please write down 2 things you can do between now and
this time tomorrow to support and encourage others.

	PLAN	ACTUAL
1		
2		

Body-*for*-LIFE   Focus on Progress, Not Perfection

Please write down 3 things you did very well today that helped
you move toward the achievement of your 12-week goals.

1	
2	
3	

Please write down one thing you will do even better tomorrow.

1	

Notes:

Body-*for*-LIFE The Eating-*for*-LIFE Method™

PLAN	ACTUAL

Meal 1

☑ a.m.
☐ p.m.

0. 3°

מחזורי
שתים
+ apple

Meal 1

☐ a.m.
☐ p.m.

Meal 2

☑ a.m.
☐ p.m.

יוגורט
דל

Meal 2

☐ a.m.
☐ p.m.

Meal 3

☑ a.m.
☐ p.m.

יוגורט
שתים

Meal 3

☐ a.m.
☐ p.m.

Meal 4

☐ a.m.
☐ p.m.

tuna
sandwich

Meal 4

☐ a.m.
☐ p.m.

Meal 5

☐ a.m.
☐ p.m.

שייק
חלב

Meal 5

☐ a.m.
☐ p.m.

Meal 6

☐ a.m.
☐ p.m.

Meal 6

☐ a.m.
☐ p.m.

Notes: מיץ w   בוקר-חלב 2 s
+ תה 2 +

Body-*for*-LIFE | The 20-Minute Aerobics Solution™

Intensity Pattern

Exercise	PLAN		ACTUAL	
	Planned Start Time: 6:30		Actual Start Time: 8:20	
	Planned End Time: 6:56		Actual End Time: 8:40	
	Time to Complete: 20 Minutes		Time to Complete: 20	
	Minute by Minute	Intensity Level	Minute by Minute	Intensity Level
recumbent b.M P3	1	5	1	
	2	5	2	
	3	6	3	
	4	7	4	
	5	8	5	
	6	9	6	
	7	6	7	
	8	7	8	
	9	8	9	
	10	9	10	
	11	6	11	
	12	7	12	
	13	8	13	
	14	9	14	
	15	6	15	
	16	7	16	
	17	8	17	
High Point	18	9	18	
	19	10	19	
	20	5	20	

Notes:

Bill Phillips | Lesson-*for*-LIFE

> "The more we work together,
> the more we can all succeed."

More and more, people are connecting with other positive, encouraging people who have decided to accept this Challenge through the Internet. The website www.BodyforLIFE.com has become a daily gathering place for people who are there to support and encourage others, and share their own lessons. Through the "guestbook," you may very well find someone who, like you, is beginning their third week of the Program, and they can share their insights, ideas, and experiences with you. And, it's very likely you have insight you can share with others. Also, I guarantee that your support and encouragement will help someone else out there who might be struggling with their Program today. Thousands of people are sharing this experience with us at this moment, and the more we work together, the more we can all succeed!

Success Story | George Nolly

Age 55•Aurora, CO•Airline Pilot
Gained 15 lbs of Muscle, Lost 25 lbs of Fat
Reduced Waist from 36 Inches to 32 Inches

As an airline pilot, I routinely use the autopilot function. Until I read Body-*for*-LIFE I hadn't realized my life had been cruising on autopilot! Although my career was very successful, my personal health was off-course. I tried to exercise and diet, but when I became a wide-body B-777 Captain, I became a "wide body" myself. I visited the Body-*for*-LIFE Web site daily, read the guestbook, and shared mini-victories with other participants. I read the success stories of others and that helped me achieve my own success.

Body-*for*-LIFE The Power Mindset

Please write down 5 things you can do between now and this time tomorrow
that will help you move forward in the direction of your 12-week goals.

PLAN	ACTUAL
1	
2	
3	
4	
5	

Body-*for*-LIFE The Universal Law of Reciprocation

Please write down 2 things you can do between now and
this time tomorrow to support and encourage others.

PLAN	ACTUAL
1	
2	

Body-*for*-LIFE Focus on Progress, Not Perfection

Please write down 3 things you did very well today that helped
you move toward the achievement of your 12-week goals.

1.
2.
3.

Please write down one thing you will do even better tomorrow.

1.

Notes:

Body-*for*-LIFE   The Eating-*for*-LIFE Method™

PLAN		ACTUAL	
Meal 1		**Meal 1**	
☑ a.m. ☐ p.m. 7:00	mesotech + appt	☑ a.m. ☐ p.m. 8:30	metrex + appt
Meal 2		**Meal 2**	
☑ a.m. ☐ p.m. 10:00	myoplx RTD	☐ a.m. ☑ p.m. 12	turkey
Meal 3		**Meal 3**	
☐ a.m. ☑ p.m. 1:00	turkey roll	☐ a.m. ☑ p.m. 3:00	tuna (½)
Meal 4		**Meal 4**	
☐ a.m. ☑ p.m. 4:00	tuna	☐ a.m. ☐ p.m. 6:00	myoplex
Meal 5		**Meal 5**	
☐ a.m. ☑ p.m.	fish + veggies myoplx	☐ a.m. ☐ p.m.	chicken soup
Meal 6		**Meal 6**	
☐ a.m. ☑ p.m.	mesotech	☐ a.m. ☐ p.m.	

Notes: phen-free x2
          phosphagen - HP

Body-*for*-LIFE — Upper Body Workout

Intensity Pattern

Planned Start Time: 6:15
Planned End Time: 6:51
Time to Complete: 46 Minutes

Actual Start Time: _____
Actual End Time: _____
Time to Complete: _____

Upper Body Muscle Groups	Exercise	Reps	Weight (lbs)	Minutes Between Sets	Intensity Level	Reps	Weight (lbs)	Minutes Between Sets	Intensity Level
Chest		12	40	1	5	12	40	1	5
	incline	10	45	1	6	12	45	1	6
	Br	8	45	1	7 2.49	8	45	1	
		6	45	1	8 42.5	6	45		7
High Point		12	45	0	9 5.51	12	45 (35)	0	8
	Fives	12	30	2	10	12	35+0	2	9
Shoulders		12	20	1	5 4.12	12	20	1	5
	military press	10	25	1	6 12.56	10	25	1	6
		8	30	1	7 14.30	8	30	1	7
		6	35	1	8 15.8	6	35	1	8
High Point	lateral raise	12	30	0	9 17.15	12	12	0	8
		12	10	2	10	12	12	2	10
Back	rows	12	40	1	5 21.0	12	12	1	5
		10	45	1	6 27.9	10	10	1	6
		8	45	1	7 24.05	8	8	1	7
		6	45	1	8 25.2	6	6	1	8
High Point	shrugs	12	45	0	9 26.4	12	12	0	8
		12	30	2	10	12	12	2	9
Triceps	tric extension	12	25	1	5 29.7	12	25	1	5
		10		1	6 31.4	10		1	6
		8		1	7	8		1	7
		6		1	8	6		1	8
High Point	dips	12		0	9	12	25	2	8
		12	12	2	10	12		2	9

At this point, you should be 37 minutes into your upper body workout and have 9 minutes to go.

Upper Body Muscle Groups	Exercise	Reps	Weight (lbs)	Minutes Between Sets	Intensity Level	Reps	Weight (lbs)	Minutes Between Sets	Intensity Level
Biceps	curls	12	25	1	5	25	12	5	5
		10	30	1	6 40	30	10	8	6
		8	35	1	7 41.0	35	8 35-2	1	7
		6	40	1	8	40	6	1	8
High Point	hammer curls	12	35	0	9	35			
		12	25	–	10	25			

Notes:
_____
_____

Bill Phillips | Lesson-*for*-LIFE

"Every transformation starts as a dream."

Your dreams and ideals are very important to your success; in fact, every transformation starts as a dream. And the more you dream of a <u>bright</u> future, the more you have to look forward to. This fuels <u>your ambit</u>ion. It's so important to keep your dreams alive and let them give you <u>the en</u>ergy and excitement that allowed you to get started in the first place. To help your success, please continually review your "Dream List," which you filled out <u>at</u> the beginning of this Program. Remember that I asked you to picture things <u>you</u>'d like to accomplish in 12 weeks—things that make you smile, things that make you feel excited, alive, optimistic, and energized! Read that Dream List and experience those emotions with as much vivid detail as possible. Think about making those dreams come true, and you'll feel the excitement, the passion, the energy you'll need to keep going strong and not give up!

Success Story | Theresa Hornick

Age 20•Villanova, PA•Student Athlete
Gained Muscle, Lost 6% Bodyfat

I had a vision of myself and what my body image could be. I just didn't know how to achieve my goals. Reading Body-*for*-LIFE gave me the answer to that "how." My greatest inspiration of all was the added confidence and positive feeling I had from seeing improvements in my body every week. A newfound inner strength has transformed my life. Attaining my best self has helped me focus on my other dreams. I realize now that I can take control of my life and make it what I want it to be.

DAY 16

Body-*for*-LIFE The Power Mindset

Please write down 5 things you can do between now and this time tomorrow
that will help you move forward in the direction of your 12-week goals.

	PLAN	ACTUAL
1		
2		
3		
4		
5		

Body-*for*-LIFE The Universal Law of Reciprocation

Please write down 2 things you can do between now and
this time tomorrow to support and encourage others.

	PLAN	ACTUAL
1		
2		

Body-*for*-LIFE Focus on Progress, Not Perfection

Please write down 3 things you did very well today that helped
you move toward the achievement of your 12-week goals.

1		
2		
3		

Please write down one thing you will do even better tomorrow.

1		

Notes:

DAY 16

Body-*for*-LIFE | The Eating-*for*-LIFE Method™

PLAN		ACTUAL	
Meal 1		**Meal 1**	
☑ a.m. ☐ p.m. 8:00	mesutch	☑ a.m. ☐ p.m.	9:46 apple
Meal 2		**Meal 2**	
☐ a.m. ☐ p.m. 11	myoplex	☐ a.m. ☐ p.m.	myoprx
Meal 3		**Meal 3**	
☐ a.m. ☐ p.m. 2	turkey	☐ a.m. ☐ p.m.	troprx
Meal 4		**Meal 4**	
☐ a.m. ☐ p.m. 5	trioplex	☐ a.m. ☐ p.m.	turky
Meal 5		**Meal 5**	
☐ a.m. ☐ p.m.	fish + salaa	☐ a.m. ☐ p.m.	cnrn salcn
Meal 6		**Meal 6**	
☐ a.m. ☐ p.m.	prco snca	☐ a.m. ☐ p.m.	paj wrln t cnrn

Notes: phen-frcc x2

Body-*for*-LIFE

The 20-Minute Aerobics Solution™

Intensity Pattern

	PLAN		ACTUAL	
Planned Start Time: 6:30			Actual Start Time: 8:26	
Planned End Time: 6:50			Actual End Time: 8:46	
Time to Complete: 20 Minutes			Time to Complete: _____	

Exercise	Minute by Minute	Intensity Level	Minute by Minute	Intensity Level
	1	5	1	5
	2	5	2	5
	3	6	3	6
	4	7	4	7
recumped	5	8	5	8
	6	9	6	9
P3	7	6	7	5
	8	7	8	6
	9	8	9	7
	10	9	10	8
	11	6	11	9
	12	7	12	5
	13	8	13	6
	14	9	14	
	15	6	15	7
	16	7	16	8
	17	8	17	9
High Point	18	9	18	9
	19	10	19	5
	20	5	20	

Notes: 5.56
388 cel
176 min → 160

DAY 17

Bill Phillips — Lesson-*for*-LIFE

> "Goals give you the ability to be
> self-directed and in control."

Reading your goals every morning and night will help you stay on course. Committing your goals to memory helps even more as it harnesses the power of a part of your mind called the "frontal cortex." Quite simply, the frontal cortex is a guidance system that directs your conscious and subconscious thoughts, patterns, and actions. Most people don't intentionally program any specific target they want to strike, which leaves the power of this part of the mind untapped. Reading and memorizing your goals every day is like giving the frontal cortex the specific directions it needs to organize your thoughts and actions, and gives you the ability to be self-directed and in control. Also, when your mind is focused on achieving specific goals, you will notice reduced stress and increased clarity, satisfaction, and peace of mind.

Success Story — Taizo Ikeda

Age 31•Montreal, QB, CAN•Mech. Designer
Gained Muscle, Lost 25 lbs of Fat

It got to the point where enough was enough... it was time to take action! I wanted to change, and I had to do this for myself. So I decided to set specific goals, and that's when everything came into place. I felt unstoppable. It's really a whole new way of living, and it's about finally losing bad habits. It's a race against time, with challenges every day, a path to follow, and a goal to reach. I feel a great sense of accomplishment by not only starting but also finishing my 12-week Program.

DAY 17

Body-*for*-LIFE The Power Mindset

Please write down 5 things you can do between now and this time tomorrow
that will help you move forward in the direction of your 12-week goals.

PLAN	ACTUAL
1	
2	
3	
4	
5	

Body-*for*-LIFE The Universal Law of Reciprocation

Please write down 2 things you can do between now and
this time tomorrow to support and encourage others.

PLAN	ACTUAL
1	
2	

Body-*for*-LIFE Focus on Progress, Not Perfection

Please write down 3 things you did very well today that helped
you move toward the achievement of your 12-week goals.

1.
2.
3.

Please write down one thing you will do even better tomorrow.

1.

Notes:

Body-*for*-LIFE The Eating-*for*-LIFE Method™

PLAN		ACTUAL	
Meal 1		**Meal 1**	
☐ a.m. ☐ p.m.	mesoTech	☐ a.m. ☐ p.m.	myoprx
Meal 2		**Meal 2**	
☐ a.m. ☐ p.m.	myoph	☐ a.m. ☑ p.m.	salmon + ves
Meal 3		**Meal 3**	
☐ a.m. ☐ p.m.	shlmn	☐ a.m. ☐ p.m.	myopha
Meal 4		**Meal 4**	
☐ a.m. ☐ p.m.	myoph	☐ a.m. ☐ p.m.	
Meal 5		**Meal 5**	
☐ a.m. ☐ p.m.	chckn po	☐ a.m. ☐ p.m.	chickn beef + ves
Meal 6		**Meal 6**	
☐ a.m. ☐ p.m.		☐ a.m. ☐ p.m.	

Notes:

Body-*for*-LIFE — Lower Body Workout

Intensity Pattern

PLAN	ACTUAL
Planned Start Time: 6:30	Actual Start Time: _____
Planned End Time: 7:12	Actual End Time: _____
Time to Complete: 42 Minutes	Time to Complete: _____

Lower Body Muscle Groups	Exercise	Reps	Weight (lbs)	Minutes Between Sets	Intensity Level	Reps	Weight (lbs)	Minutes Between Sets	Intensity Level
Quads	ex7	12	120	45'1	5	12	120	45'	5
		10	125	1	6	10	125	45'	6
		8	125	1	7 2.09	8	125	45"	7
		6	125	1	8 2.11	6	125	45'	8
High Point	squats	12	125	0	9	12	125	0	
		12	90	2	10	12	90	2	
Hamstrings	curls	12	60	1	5 2.25	12	60	1	5
		10	65	1	6	10	65	1	6
		8	70	1	7	8	70	1	7
		6	75	1	8 1.34?	6	75	1	8
High Point	lunges	12	70	0	9 15.15	12	70	0	9
		12	35	2	10	12	35	2	9
Calves	angry calf extension	12	40	1 20.05	5	12	40	1	6
		10	45	1	6	10 22.?	45	1	6
		8	45	1	7	8	45	1	8
		6	45	1	8	6	45	1	8
High Point		12	45	0	9 26.1	12	45	0	3
		12	40	2	10	12	40	2	3

At this point, you should be 31 minutes into your lower body workout and have 11 minutes to go.

Lower Body Muscle Groups	Exercise	Reps	Weight (lbs)	Minutes Between Sets	Intensity Level	Reps	Weight (lbs)	Minutes Between Sets	Intensity Level
Abs	Dalms b+1	12	0	1	5	12	0	1	5
		10		1	6 32"	10		1	6
		8		1	7 34"	8		1	7
		6		1	8	6 36		1	8
High Point		12		0	9 37.?	12		1	3
	exp	12		–	10	12		1	8

Notes:

_____

_____

_____

_____

_____

_____

Bill Phillips — Lesson-*for*-LIFE

"Planning overrides procrastination."

What I've discovered is that one of the reasons people put off, postpone, and procrastinate is simply because they're not prepared. Quite often, that's what it comes down to. And while the stereotypical advice, "Stop procrastinating!" certainly has merit and may be offered with the best of intentions, the solution is conspicuously absent. How *do* you stop procrastinating? How do you, "Just do it!"? What I've discovered is that procrastination is a "side effect" of a lack of preparation and planning. By "preparation," I mean gathering the essential information and acquiring the knowledge you need to accomplish your goals. And by "planning," I mean deciding how and when you will *apply* the information you've acquired. When you are prepared and you have a plan, you will not procrastinate. You will move forward and you will "just do it," because you've prepared to do it and planned to do it!

Success Story — Erin Lindsey

**Age 25 • Westland, MI • MBA Student/Asst. Mgr.
Increased Energy, Gained 7 lbs of Muscle**

The discipline it takes to finish this Program has spilled over into other areas of my life. A habitual procrastinator, I have become a more organized person, attacking things head on today, rather than a few days down the road. I also have more strength and energy to handle life's everyday stresses. I encourage everyone to try the Body-*for*-LIFE Program and find out how strong they really are! I wish everyone could feel the rewards of strengthening their mind, body, and spirit as I have.

Body-*for*-LIFE   The Power Mindset

Please write down 5 things you can do between now and this time tomorrow
that will help you move forward in the direction of your 12-week goals.

	PLAN	ACTUAL
1		
2		
3		
4		
5		

Body-*for*-LIFE   The Universal Law of Reciprocation

Please write down 2 things you can do between now and
this time tomorrow to support and encourage others.

	PLAN	ACTUAL
1		
2		

Body-*for*-LIFE   Focus on Progress, Not Perfection

Please write down 3 things you did very well today that helped
you move toward the achievement of your 12-week goals.

1	
2	
3	

Please write down one thing you will do even better tomorrow.

1	

Notes:

DAY 18

Body-*for*-LIFE   The Eating-*for*-LIFE Method™

PLAN	ACTUAL

Meal 1

☐ a.m. ☐ p.m.   myoplex ↑ appn

Meal 1

☐ a.m. ☐ p.m.   myoplx

Meal 2

☐ a.m. ☐ p.m.   tuna

Meal 2

☐ a.m. ☐ p.m.   tuna

Meal 3

☐ a.m. ☐ p.m.   myoplex

Meal 3

☐ a.m. ☐ p.m.   myoplx

Meal 4

☐ a.m. ☐ p.m.   trioplx

Meal 4

☐ a.m. ☐ p.m.   tuna

Meal 5

☐ a.m. ☐ p.m.   Fish

Meal 5

☐ a.m. ☐ p.m.   mat ffuls x2

Meal 6

☐ a.m. ☐ p.m.   mentca

Meal 6

☐ a.m. ☐ p.m.   myo

Notes: _____

Body-*for*-LIFE | The 20-Minute Aerobics Solution™

Intensity Pattern

Exercise	PLAN		ACTUAL	
	Planned Start Time: 6:05		Actual Start Time:	
	Planned End Time: 6:25		Actual End Time:	
	Time to Complete: 20 Minutes		Time to Complete:	
	Minute by Minute	Intensity Level	Minute by Minute	Intensity Level
recumbent p.m. Ⓑ	1	5	1	5
	2	5	2	6
	3	6	3	7
	4	7	4	8
	5	8	5	
	6	9	6	9
	7	6	7	5
	8	7	8	
	9	8	9	6
	10	9	10	7
	11	6	11	
	12	7	12	8
	13	8	13	8
	14	9	14	
	15	6	15	5
	16	7	16	6
	17	8	17	7
High Point	18	9	18	8
	19	10	19	9
	20	5	20	10

Notes: 21''   176 — 156   5

3 16 ccl

Bill Phillips Lesson-*for*-LIFE

"Start driving, and stop just going along for the ride."

I don't know anyone who can honestly tell me they ended up in poor physical condition, overweight, or weak on purpose. It's something that happens unintentionally. Oftentimes, when people focus their attention on their careers, their education, or dealing with a life crisis, they put their health and fitness on "cruise control." They let go of the steering wheel and take their eyes off the road. Before long, their physical condition and health are completely off track. The style of living that causes poor health is not that complicated to understand. And, fortunately, neither is the process of getting back on track. But you have to disconnect the cruise control, put both hands on the wheel, and focus your vision on where you want to go. You have to start driving, and stop just going along for the ride. You have to *intentionally* undo the things that happened *accidentally*.

Success Story Chris Whitman

**Age 34•Glendale, AZ•Father/Contractor
Gained 5 lbs of Muscle, Lost 32 lbs of Fat**

I was 30 lbs overweight, and my relationship with my wife and children was suffering. I made the decision to change and promised my wife things were going to be different. Through the Program, I transformed myself from a person who didn't care to a person who is committed to the self-improvement of himself and others. I have been blessed with new feelings of compassion for others. I believe this Program is all about winning at life. My past has been put to rest, and I'm excited about creating my future!

Body-*for*-LIFE   The Power Mindset

Please write down 5 things you can do between now and this time tomorrow that will help you move forward in the direction of your 12-week goals.

	PLAN	ACTUAL
1		
2		
3		
4		
5		

Body-*for*-LIFE   The Universal Law of Reciprocation

Please write down 2 things you can do between now and this time tomorrow to support and encourage others.

	PLAN	ACTUAL
1		
2		

Body-*for*-LIFE   Focus on Progress, Not Perfection

Please write down 3 things you did very well today that helped you move toward the achievement of your 12-week goals.

1	
2	
3	

Please write down one thing you will do even better tomorrow.

1	

Notes:

Body-*for*-LIFE — The Eating-*for*-LIFE Method™

PLAN		ACTUAL	
Meal 1		**Meal 1**	
⊘ a.m. ☐ p.m.	mesolech	☐ a.m. ☐ p.m.	myopin
Meal 2		**Meal 2**	
☑ a.m. ☐ p.m.	½ ₸₸₸₸₸₸	☐ a.m. ☐ p.m.	½ Tum
Meal 3		**Meal 3**	
☐ a.m. ☐ p.m.	(fish)	☐ a.m. ☐ p.m.	₸₸₸₸ ₸ xm
Meal 4		**Meal 4**	
☐ a.m. ☐ p.m.	mygyplea ₸₸₸	☐ a.m. ☐ p.m.	2 courgea +
Meal 5		**Meal 5**	½ coin
☐ a.m. ☐ p.m.	chrchs	☐ a.m. ☐ p.m.	
Meal 6		**Meal 6**	
☐ a.m. ☐ p.m.	,myupur ₸₸₸₸₸	☐ a.m. ☐ p.m.	mesolece

Notes:

Body-*for*-LIFE | Upper Body Workout

Intensity Pattern

Planned Start Time: 6:15

Planned End Time: 7:00

Time to Complete: 46 Minutes

Actual Start Time: _____

Actual End Time: _____

Time to Complete: _____

Upper Body Muscle Groups	Exercise	Reps	Weight (lbs)	Minutes Between Sets	Intensity Level	Reps	Weight (lbs)	Minutes Between Sets	Intensity Level
Chest	incln dumbbll c...	12	40	1	5	12	40	1	5
		10	45	1	6	10	45	1	6
		8	45	1	7 2:3	8	45	1	7
		6	45	1	8	6	45	1	8
High Point		12	45	0	9 5:00	12	40-30	0	9
		12	35	2	10	12	35-30	2	9
Shoulders	military pres	12	25	1	5	12	25	1	5
		10	30	1	6 12:0	10	30 8:43	1	6
		8	35	1	7	8	35	1	7
		6	40	1	8 15:26	6	40	1	8
High Point	clean	12	35	0	9 19:?	12	35	0	9
		12	10	2	10	12	10	2	8
Back		12	40	1	5 12:0	12	40	1	8
		10	45	1	6 22:?	10	45	1	6
		8	45	1	7 23:22	8	45	1	7
		6	45	1	8 25:40	6	45	1	8
High Point		12	45	0	9 27:40	12	45	0	8
		12	25	2	10	12	25	2	8
Triceps	extens	12	25	1	5	12	25	1	5
		10		1	6	10		1	6
		8		1	7	8		1	7
		6		1	8	6		1	8
High Point	clay	12	25	0	9	12			8
		12	10	2	10	12	8 - 4 PL		8

At this point, you should be 37 minutes into your upper body workout and have 9 minutes to go.

Upper Body Muscle Groups	Exercise	Reps	Weight (lbs)	Minutes Between Sets	Intensity Level	Reps	Weight (lbs)	Minutes Between Sets	Intensity Level
Biceps		12	20	1	5	12	20	1	5
		10	25	1	6	10	25	1	6
		8	30	1	7 41?	8	30	1	9
		6	35	1	8 43:06	6	35	1	
High Point		12	30	0	9 44:37	12	30	0	
		12	25	–	10	12		2	

Notes: _____

_____

_____

Bill Phillips | Lesson-*for*-LIFE

"Are you in or are you out?"

By this point in the Program, some people have already quit. Their goals weren't meaningful, and, quite frankly, they never really decided to make a change for the better. What about you? Are you ready to give up? Or are you going to continue on and become a success story? Of course, you know by now I care about you, and I want you to succeed, but I can't make you do it if you don't really want to. Just be honest with yourself—if you're not committed to finishing, stick a fork in it already. Here's how: simply write the words, "I quit!" on the cover of this book, in big, bold print, and sign your name under it. Then, send it to me: Bill Phillips, PO Box 16009, Golden, CO 80402. I'll send you a check for the cover price of this *Success Journal*. Fair enough?

Success Story | Everett Herbert

Age 53•Holladay, UT•Contractor
Gained 10 lbs of Muscle, Lost 15 lbs of Fat

One of the main things that kept me going when that voice in my head was screaming, "Quit!" was that I knew in my heart that finishing this one workout today would determine who I was, what I would look like, and how I would feel about myself tomorrow. I didn't want to be a quitter anymore. I wanted to be a success! And so I never gave up. I never quit and that feeling that I can succeed came back. For me, the physical change is only a metaphor for the really important changes that took place in my life.

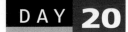

DAY 20

Body-*for*-LIFE — The Power Mindset

Please write down 5 things you can do between now and this time tomorrow that will help you move forward in the direction of your 12-week goals.

	PLAN	ACTUAL
1		
2		
3		
4		
5		

Body-*for*-LIFE — The Universal Law of Reciprocation

Please write down 2 things you can do between now and this time tomorrow to support and encourage others.

	PLAN	ACTUAL
1		
2		

Body-*for*-LIFE — Focus on Progress, Not Perfection

Please write down 3 things you did very well today that helped you move toward the achievement of your 12-week goals.

1	
2	
3	

Please write down one thing you will do even better tomorrow.

1	

Notes:

Body-*for*-LIFE | The Eating-*for*-LIFE Method™

PLAN		ACTUAL	
Meal 1		**Meal 1**	
☐ a.m. ☐ p.m.		☐ a.m. ☐ p.m.	
Meal 2		**Meal 2**	
☐ a.m. ☐ p.m.		☐ a.m. ☐ p.m.	
Meal 3		**Meal 3**	
☐ a.m. ☐ p.m.		☐ a.m. ☐ p.m.	
Meal 4		**Meal 4**	
☐ a.m. ☐ p.m.		☐ a.m. ☐ p.m.	
Meal 5		**Meal 5**	
☐ a.m. ☐ p.m.		☐ a.m. ☐ p.m.	
Meal 6		**Meal 6**	
☐ a.m. ☐ p.m.		☐ a.m. ☐ p.m.	

Notes:

Body-*for*-LIFE

The 20-Minute Aerobics Solution™

Intensity Pattern

		PLAN		ACTUAL	
	Planned Start Time: 8'00			Actual Start Time: 8:50	
	Planned End Time: 8.2>			Actual End Time: 3:10	
	Time to Complete: 20 Minutes			Time to Complete: _____	
Exercise	**Minute by Minute**	**Intensity Level**		**Minute by Minute**	**Intensity Level**
	1	5		1	5
	2	5		2	6
	3	6		3	7
recumbw	4	7		4	8
bins	5	8		5	9
P3	6	9		6	5
	7	6		7	
	8	7		8	6
	9	8		9	7
	10	9		10	
	11	6		11	8
	12	7		12	9
	13	8		13	5
	14	9		14	6
	15	6		15	7
	16	7		16	8
	17	8		17	
High Point	18	9		18	9
	180 19	10		19	10
	170 20	5		20	5

Notes: HR 181 → 170

38 5.

38J cu

Bill Phillips | Lesson-*for*-LIFE

> "Measure success by what you gain,
> not by what you lose."

I cannot emphasize enough that the Body-*for*-LIFE Program is not simply about weight loss. Unlike virtually all the popular diet programs that basically measure your success by how much less space you take up on the planet, Body-*for*-LIFE is different: It's about gaining energy, increasing strength, renewing health, *and* decreasing bodyfat. So please, don't make the mistake of measuring your success each day, each week, or each month by the amount of weight a scale says you have lost. Measure your success by what you gain, not by what you lose: Gaining strength. Gaining muscle. Gaining energy. Gaining self-respect. Gaining self-awareness. Gaining self-trust. Gaining self-esteem. Gaining back control of your life! This is what the Body-*for*-LIFE experience is all about!

Success Story | Russell and Teri Mason

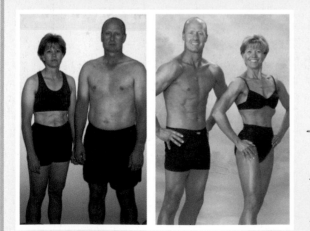

Ages 42 and 40 • Aurora, UT
Coal Miner and Cosmetology Instructor
Combined Lost 54 lbs of Fat
Gained 21 lbs of Muscle

In the past, we identified losing weight as the reward for exercise. We now believe that mental clarity is the greatest reward, and we have never thought so clearly. We have a new sense of faith, of hope, and a belief that we are capable. We have more energy to give to each other and to our children. We never envisioned a decision to be healthy could have such a dramatic effect on our lives. We now realize what a great gift our son gave us when he introduced us to Body-*for*-LIFE and encouraged us to do it.

Body-*for*-LIFE   The Power Mindset

Please write down 5 things you can do between now and this time tomorrow
that will help you move forward in the direction of your 12-week goals.

	PLAN	ACTUAL
1	use money to pay down debt of credit cards to saving B...	
2		
3		
4		
5		

Body-*for*-LIFE   The Universal Law of Reciprocation

Please write down 2 things you can do between now and
this time tomorrow to support and encourage others.

	PLAN	ACTUAL
1		
2		

Body-*for*-LIFE   Focus on Progress, Not Perfection

Please write down 3 things you did very well today that helped
you move toward the achievement of your 12-week goals.

1	
2	
3	

Please write down one thing you will do even better tomorrow.

1	

Notes:

DAY 22

Body-for-LIFE — The Eating-for-LIFE Method™

PLAN		ACTUAL	
Meal 1		**Meal 1**	
7:15 ☑a.m. ☐p.m.	protein shum phosphage	☐a.m. ☐p.m.	
Meal 2		**Meal 2**	
10:00 ☑p.m. ☐a.m.	trioplex or 2 meostuck	☐a.m. ☐p.m.	
Meal 3		**Meal 3**	
1:00 ☑p.m. ☐a.m.	½ tuna ~~aast.~~	☐a.m. ☐p.m.	
Meal 4		**Meal 4**	
☑p.m. ☐a.m.	½ trioplex & ½ tuna	☐a.m. ☐p.m.	
Meal 5		**Meal 5**	
☑p.m. ☐a.m.	fonicham t vg	☐a.m. ☐p.m.	
Meal 6		**Meal 6**	
☑p.m. ☐a.m.	potein shck	☐a.m. ☐p.m.	

Notes: 17Sb   phen-free x2

phosphage 2 ru t 250ml or wtr

Body-*for*-LIFE — Lower Body Workout

Intensity Pattern

	PLAN	ACTUAL
	Planned Start Time: 6:15	Actual Start Time: 7:15
	Planned End Time: 6:58	Actual End Time: 8:00
	Time to Complete: 42 Minutes	Time to Complete: 42"

Lower Body Muscle Groups	Exercise	Reps	Weight (lbs)	Minutes Between Sets	Intensity Level	Reps	Weight (lbs)	Minutes Between Sets	Intensity Level
Quads	quad	12	120	1	5	12	120	1	5
	ext	10	125	1	6	10	125	1	6
		8	125	1	7 2:8"	8	125	1	7
		6	125	1	8 4	6	125	1	8
High Point	squat	12	125	0	9	12	120	0	9
		12	90	2	10	12	125	2	9
Hamstrings	curls	12	50	1	5 3:45	12	50	1	5
		10	55	1	6	10	55	1	6
		8	60	1	7 13:2"	8	60	1	7
		6	65	1	8	6	65	1	8
High Point	lunge	12	60	0	9 16:5"	12	60	1	9
		12	35	2	10	12	35	1	10
Calves	2x7	12	40	1	5	12	40	1	5
		10	45	1	6	10	45	1	6
		8	45	1	7	8	41	1	7
		6	45	1	8	6	45	1	8
High Point		12	45	0	9	12	45	2	8
		12	90	2	10	12	30	2	8

At this point, you should be 31 minutes into your lower body workout and have 11 minutes to go.

		Reps	Weight (lbs)	Minutes Between Sets	Intensity Level	Reps	Weight (lbs)	Minutes Between Sets	Intensity Level
Abs	bell	12	12	1	5	12	12	1	5
	crun	10	10	1	6 3"	10	10	1	6
		8	8	1	7 3:4	8	8	1	7
		6	6	1	8	6	6	1	8
High Point		12	12	0	9 3:7:3	12	12	0	9
	scxos crun	12	12	–	10	12	12	2	10

Notes: 1 by 5 lb. T. 125 - shorten no break.
T. 45x ... or bug run w-lur gru

Bill Phillips — Lesson-*for*-LIFE

"Open up and give it all you've got!"

You're now into your fourth week of the Program, and you're experienced enough that you can take it up a notch—there's no reason to be tentative. You know the workouts, the nutrition, the mind-set exercises. You also know why you're doing this Program and what you want out of it. You know what you need to know to successfully transform. So don't be afraid to open up and give it all you've got! I know you have the power to change. Now is the time to unleash even more of that power! Hit higher high points, follow your nutrition plan, complete your daily goals, transform your patterns of action. Don't be afraid to trust yourself. Don't hold back! From this day forward, you will notice your workouts are more intense, healthy food tastes even better, planning and recording your daily activities will be even easier, and your energy will rise!

Success Story — Scott Randles

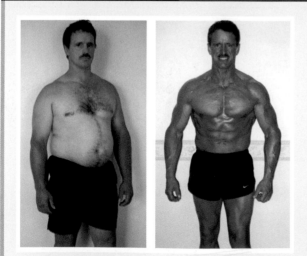

Age 43 • Enumclaw, WA • Logger Crew Leader
Lost 56 lbs of Fat, Gained 9 lbs of Muscle
Reduced Bodyfat from 29% to 7%

I caught a reflection of my fat body in a mirror and I was shocked. The man I saw got that way through excuses and neglect. That realization served as the inspiration for me to make a change. Day by day, I stopped making excuses and started making changes. I followed the Body-*for*-LIFE Program and gave it 100%! The transformation I experienced has crossed over into all aspects of my life. Without a doubt, physically, mentally, and emotionally, I am now stronger and better!

DAY **23**

Body-*for*-LIFE   The Power Mindset

Please write down 5 things you can do between now and this time tomorrow
that will help you move forward in the direction of your 12-week goals.

	PLAN	ACTUAL
1		
2		
3		
4		
5		

Body-*for*-LIFE   The Universal Law of Reciprocation

Please write down 2 things you can do between now and
this time tomorrow to support and encourage others.

	PLAN	ACTUAL
1		
2		

Body-*for*-LIFE   Focus on Progress, Not Perfection

Please write down 3 things you did very well today that helped
you move toward the achievement of your 12-week goals.

1	
2	
3	

Please write down one thing you will do even better tomorrow.

1	

Notes:

DAY 23

Body-for-LIFE — The Eating-for-LIFE Method™

PLAN	ACTUAL

Meal 1

PLAN: ☑ a.m. ☐ p.m. 7:0-
protein
shuli
1 photosphism

ACTUAL: ☑ a.m. ☐ p.m. 8:45
mesoteen
myoplex

Meal 2

PLAN: ☐ a.m. ☐ p.m.
protein
ps-

ACTUAL: ☐ a.m. ☐ p.m. 11:00
myoplus

Meal 3

PLAN: ☐ a.m. ☐ p.m.
tuna

ACTUAL: ☐ a.m. ☐ p.m.
turkey

Meal 4

PLAN: ☐ a.m. ☐ p.m.
protein
shin

ACTUAL: ☐ a.m. ☐ p.m.
turkey

Meal 5

PLAN: ☐ a.m. ☐ p.m.
fish/veg

ACTUAL: ☐ a.m. ☐ p.m.

Meal 6

PLAN: ☐ a.m. ☐ p.m.
protein
shin

ACTUAL: ☐ a.m. ☐ p.m.
salmon
+
veggi

Notes: w? 172.5 lb

Body-*for*-LIFE | The 20-Minute Aerobics Solution™

Intensity Pattern

Exercise	PLAN		ACTUAL	
	PLAN		**ACTUAL**	
	Planned Start Time: 6:05		Actual Start Time: 7:30	
	Planned End Time: 6:30		Actual End Time: 8:50	
	Time to Complete: 20 Minutes		Time to Complete: _____	
	Minute by Minute	Intensity Level	Minute by Minute	Intensity Level
recumbent bicycle	1	5	1	5
	2	5	2	6
	3	6	3	7
	4	7	4	8
	5	8	5	9
	6	9	6	5
	7	6	7	6
	8	7	8	7
	9	8	9	8
	10	9	10	9
	11	6	11	5
	12	7	12	6
	13	8	13	7
	14	9	14	8
	15	6	15	9
	16	7	16	9
	17	8	17	9
High Point	18	9	18	10
	19	10	19	
	20	5	20	5

Notes: 181
5.78
321 N 4

Bill Phillips — Lesson-*for*-LIFE

> "The heart of Body-*for*-LIFE
> is developing self-trust."

As you're discovering, Body-*for*-LIFE is about much more than working out and eating right: It's about developing character as much as it is about developing muscle. At the heart of the Body-*for*-LIFE Program is developing self-trust, self-respect, and self-esteem. Each day you set your goals and honor your self-promises, you'll notice renewed self-confidence and pride!

Success Story — Randy Penberthy

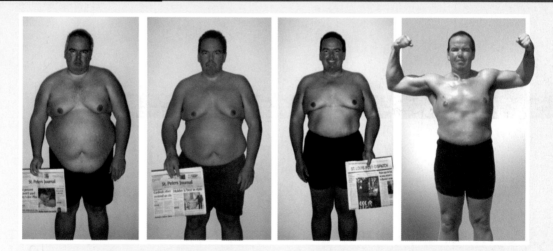

**Age 41•St. Peters, MO• Manager, Systems Development
Completed Three 12-Week Programs, Lost 184 lbs**

My life had been plagued with broken promises and unfulfilled dreams, but through the successes found by staying with the Program, I learned the value of honoring my promises. I lost 184 lbs after finishing 3 consecutive Body-*for*-LIFE Programs. I started at 368 lbs and finished at 184 lbs. My bodyfat percentage dropped from 56% to below 15%. My waistline dropped from 62 to 34. Instead of my previous belligerent personality, attempting to mask a fear of rejection and low self-esteem, I now possess a quieter demeanor, yet with profound inner strength and peace. I have experienced firsthand the positive physical and emotional changes triggered by the process of building a strong, healthy body.

Body-*for*-LIFE The Power Mindset

Please write down 5 things you can do between now and this time tomorrow that will help you move forward in the direction of your 12-week goals.

	PLAN	ACTUAL
1		
2		
3		
4		
5		

Body-*for*-LIFE The Universal Law of Reciprocation

Please write down 2 things you can do between now and this time tomorrow to support and encourage others.

	PLAN	ACTUAL
1		
2		

Body-*for*-LIFE Focus on Progress, Not Perfection

Please write down 3 things you did very well today that helped you move toward the achievement of your 12-week goals.

1	— working hard – complying tm. o rpn rummmc BOD3 FUR LIFt pnjm 1 p1
2	
3	

Please write down one thing you will do even better tomorrow.

1	

Notes:

Body-*for*-LIFE The Eating-*for*-LIFE Method™

PLAN	ACTUAL

Meal 1

☑ a.m.
☐ p.m.
8:15

(handwritten, circled) mesotcch snalt + uppt

Meal 1

☐ a.m.
☐ p.m.

Mesotcch ᴛ uppt

Meal 2

☑ a.m.
☐ p.m.
10:30

nny-plr smin

Meal 2

☐ a.m.
☐ p.m.

sensun pota pur

Meal 3

☐ a.m.
☑ p.m.
7

funs

Meal 3

☐ a.m.
☐ p.m.

Meal 4

☐ a.m.
☐ p.m.

½ Tropter

Meal 4

☐ a.m.
☐ p.m.

myophx

Meal 5

☐ a.m.
☐ p.m.

FLUW fin

Meal 5

☐ a.m.
☐ p.m.

rea nupph saiti

Meal 6

☐ a.m.
☐ p.m.

Meal 6

☐ a.m.
☐ p.m.

Notes: pnn-fm

Body-for-LIFE — Upper Body Workout

Intensity Pattern

	PLAN	ACTUAL
Planned Start Time: 7:14		Actual Start Time: 7:30
Planned End Time: 8:00		Actual End Time: 8:16
Time to Complete: 46 Minutes		Time to Complete: 47'

Upper Body Muscle Groups	Exercise	Reps	Weight (lbs)	Minutes Between Sets	Intensity Level	Reps	Weight (lbs)	Minutes Between Sets	Intensity Level
Chest	incln	12	40	1	5	12	40	1	5
	BP	10	45	1	6	10	45	1	6
		8	45	1	7	8	45	1	7
		6	45	1	8	6	45	1	8
High Point	flys	12	45	0	9	12	45	0	9
		12	30	2	10	12	3.0	2	8
Shoulders	press	12	20	1	5	12	20	1	5
		10	25	1	6	10	25	1	6
		8	30	1	7	8	30	1	7
		6	35	1	8	6	35	1	6
High Point	lat rs	12	30	0	9	12	20	0	8
		12	10	2	10	12	11	2	8
Back	rows	12	40	1	5	12	40	1	5
		10	45	1	6	10	45	1	6
		8	45	1	7	8		1	7
		6	45	1	8	6		1	8
High Point	srows	12	45	0	9	12	45	0	9
		12	30	2	10	12		2	8
Triceps	ext	12	25	1	5	12	25	1	5
		10		1	6	12		1	6
		8		1	7	12		1	7
		6		1	8	12		1	8
High Point	ext	12		0	9	12 (2) 25		0	8
		12		2	10	12		2	9

At this point, you should be 37 minutes into your upper body workout and have 9 minutes to go.

Upper Body Muscle Groups	Exercise	Reps	Weight (lbs)	Minutes Between Sets	Intensity Level	Reps	Weight (lbs)	Minutes Between Sets	Intensity Level
Biceps	curl	12	25	1	5	25	12	1	5
		10	30	1	6	30	10		6
		8	35	1	7	35	8		7
		6	40	1	8	40	6		8
High Point	hammer curl	12	35	0	9	35 30 25 20 12			9
		12	25	–	10	20	12		9

Notes: bench pm -ccvr Arm NYSx.

Bill Phillips Lesson-*for*-LIFE

"Keeping your goals in sight will help you succeed!"

When I talk about success, again and again you'll hear me talk about goals. Setting them *and* focusing on them daily is so important. A simple but very effective way to keep your goals in sight is to write them down on "sticky notes" and put them in places where you'll see them often, such as on a bathroom mirror, on the corner of your computer screen, on your refrigerator door, on the control panel of your home-exercise stationary bike or StairMaster. Please don't make the mistake of setting your goals and writing them down at the beginning of your Program and then not looking at them again until the end. When your written goals are out of sight, they're usually out of mind. Keeping your goals in sight, and reading them over and over again, will help you stay focused and will help you succeed!

Success Story Lezlee Jones

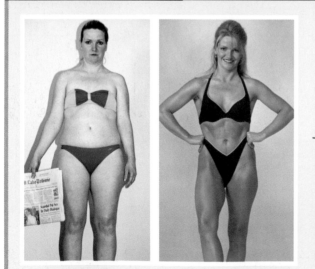

**Age 38 • Bountiful, UT • Hairstylist
Increased Strength, Lost over 30 lbs of Fat**

On the day I decided to accept this Challenge, I took responsibility for my own health and happiness. Through the 12-week Program, I discovered I have the power to let go of the negativity in my past. I proved that I'm capable of accomplishing whatever I set my mind to. Now when I give my children that speech about how "you can achieve your goals in life and be whoever you want to be," I don't feel like a hypocrite, because instead of just saying it, they've watched me do it—they've watched me succeed!

Body-*for*-LIFE   The Power Mindset

Please write down 5 things you can do between now and this time tomorrow
that will help you move forward in the direction of your 12-week goals.

	PLAN	ACTUAL
1		
2		
3		
4		
5		

Body-*for*-LIFE   The Universal Law of Reciprocation

Please write down 2 things you can do between now and
this time tomorrow to support and encourage others.

	PLAN	ACTUAL
1		
2		

Body-*for*-LIFE   Focus on Progress, Not Perfection

Please write down 3 things you did very well today that helped
you move toward the achievement of your 12-week goals.

1	
2	
3	

Please write down one thing you will do even better tomorrow.

1	

Notes:

DAY 25

Body-*for*-LIFE — The Eating-*for*-LIFE Method™

PLAN		ACTUAL	
Meal 1		**Meal 1**	
☑ a.m. ☐ p.m. 7:	גרעינים שמן זית	☐ a.m. ☐ p.m.	mesotech 7 apple
Meal 2		**Meal 2**	
☐ a.m. ☐ p.m.	מ'רקות	☐ a.m. ☑ p.m. 12:10	tuna
Meal 3		**Meal 3**	
☐ a.m. ☐ p.m.	tuna	☐ a.m. ☑ p.m.	3. tuna 2
Meal 4		**Meal 4**	
☐ a.m. ☐ p.m.	מרקות	☐ a.m. ☑ p.m. 6:00	fin/salad ירקות
Meal 5		**Meal 5**	
☐ a.m. ☐ p.m.	fin/salad ברכ	☐ a.m. ☑ p.m. 8:30	mesotech
Meal 6		**Meal 6**	
☐ a.m. ☐ p.m.	חלבון חלמא	☐ a.m. ☐ p.m.	

Notes: שתיה (פעם x 2)

Body-*for*-LIFE

The 20-Minute Aerobics Solution™

Intensity Pattern

	PLAN		ACTUAL	
Planned Start Time: 6:05			**Actual Start Time:** 6:50	
Planned End Time: 6:25			**Actual End Time:** 7:10	
Time to Complete: 20 Minutes			**Time to Complete:** 20	

Exercise	Minute by Minute	Intensity Level	Minute by Minute	Intensity Level
	1	5	1	8
	2	5	2	8
	3	6	3	7
	4	7	4	8
	5	8	5	9
RECUMBENT	6	9	6	5
BIKE	7	6	7	6
P3	8	7	8	7
	9	8	9	8
	10	9	10	9
20	11	6	11	5
	12	7	12	6
	13	8	13	7
	14	9	14	
	15	6	15	8
	16	7	16	
	17	8	17	9
High Point	18	9	18	9
	19	10	19	
	20	5	20	5

Notes: 170 bp

Bill Phillips — Lesson-*for*-LIFE

"Nourish your body each and every day."

You don't have to use nutritional supplements to complete this Program. However, if you are determined to make a remarkable transformation in only 12 weeks, you must nourish your body daily, with the quality protein, carbohydrates, essential fats, vitamins, minerals, and water your body needs to recover from your intense workouts. Remember that exercise increases your body's need for nutrients, and without optimal levels, you will not be able to maximize the fat-burning or muscle-strengthening effects of exercise. When you exercise a nutrient-deficient body, you're not making it healthier, you're actually creating a worse nutrient deficiency. That's one reason people often feel tired and run-down when they start exercising but don't eat right. So please, be sure to feed your body the nutrients it needs each and *every* day, whether you use supplements or not.

Success Story — Scott Bequette

Age 37 • Riverton, UT • Home Builder
Reduced Waist Size from 38" to 32"

When I began the Program, I had to completely change my nutrition. I began eating three healthy, whole-food meals and three Myoplex™ nutrition shakes every day. I now have more strength and energy during my workouts and while I'm at work. And I no longer get tired in the middle of the day. I found that by sticking with the Body-*for*-LIFE nutrition method, I was able to stay more focused, which helped me successfully complete the Challenge. I am now a new and improved version of my old self!

Body-*for*-LIFE   The Power Mindset

Please write down 5 things you can do between now and this time tomorrow
that will help you move forward in the direction of your 12-week goals.

	PLAN	ACTUAL
1		
2		
3		
4		
5		

Body-*for*-LIFE   The Universal Law of Reciprocation

Please write down 2 things you can do between now and
this time tomorrow to support and encourage others.

	PLAN	ACTUAL
1		
2		

Body-*for*-LIFE   Focus on Progress, Not Perfection

Please write down 3 things you did very well today that helped
you move toward the achievement of your 12-week goals.

1	
2	
3	

Please write down one thing you will do even better tomorrow.

1	

Notes:

DAY 26

Body-for-LIFE The Eating-for-LIFE Method™

PLAN		ACTUAL	
Meal 1		**Meal 1**	
☐ a.m. ☐ p.m.	*myores 1 c/r*	☐ a.m. ☐ p.m.	*mevied + mysprx + grm*
Meal 2		**Meal 2**	
☐ a.m. ☐ p.m.	*1*	☐ a.m. ☐ p.m.	*mysupn*
Meal 3		**Meal 3**	
☐ a.m. ☐ p.m.	*fish + sem*	*1* ☐ a.m. ☐ p.m.	*sermins sem trun trlal*
Meal 4		**Meal 4**	
☐ a.m. ☐ p.m.	*turky*	*4* ☐ a.m. ☐ p.m.	*turm whell 67*
Meal 5		**Meal 5**	
☐ a.m. ☐ p.m.	*mysfn*	*7* ☐ a.m. ☐ p.m.	*2 turm*
Meal 6		**Meal 6**	
☐ a.m. ☐ p.m.	*f sh 7 sh*	*9cu* ☐ a.m. ☐ p.m.	*fish-realn ½ p + purvrxn + ½ pm*

Notes: *panfurr*

Body-*for*-LIFE   Lower Body Workout

Intensity Pattern

	PLAN	ACTUAL
	Planned Start Time: 6:04	Actual Start Time: 6:30
	Planned End Time: 4:49	Actual End Time: 7:12
	Time to Complete: 42 Minutes	Time to Complete: 30"

Lower Body Muscle Groups	Exercise	Reps	Weight (lbs)	Minutes Between Sets	Intensity Level	Reps	Weight (lbs)	Minutes Between Sets	Intensity Level
Quads	extens.	12	120	1	5	120	120	1	5
		10	125	1	6	120	125	1	6
		8	125	1	7 2:41	15	125	1	7
		6	125	1	8 4.26	6	125	1	8
High Point	squat	12	125	0	9 5.54	12	125	0	9
		12	90	2	10	12	90	2	9
Hamstrings	curls	12	55	1	5 9:5	12	55	1	5
		10	60	1	6 11:4	10	60	1	6
		8	65	1	7	8 13.3'	65	1	7
		6	70	1	8 15.4	6	70	1	8
High Point	lunge.	12	65	0	9 29	12	65 69/42	0	9
		12	35	2	10	12	35	2	9
Calves	extens.	12	40	1	5 22.4	12	40	1	6
		10	45	1	6	10	45	1	7
		8	45	1	7 25.2	8	45	1	8
		6	45	1	8	6	45	1	9
High Point		12	45	0	9 27	12	45	0	9
		12	35	2	10	12	(30)	2	9

At this point, you should be 31 minutes into your lower body workout and have 11 minutes to go.

Abs		12	12	1	5	12	8	12	5
	reverse	10	10	1	6	10		10	6
	crunche	8	8	1	7	8		30"	7
		6	6	1	8	6		35	8
High Point	bell crunch	12	12	0	9	12		12	9
		12	12	–	10	12		12	9

Notes: leave curls the same
– buy more ways for ext. or quad
                                    30 to 35

Bill Phillips — Lesson-*for*-LIFE

"Success is earning it, not just owning it."

I often hear talk about the idea that science might someday develop a "magic pill" that will help people transform their bodies from fat to fit without any work at all. On the surface, that might sound like a good thing; however, beneath the surface, I think that would be one of the worst inventions of modern science. In a way, it would be like receiving a college diploma without ever having to go to class or do homework. You see, it's the *earning* of a diploma that defines success, not just the *owning* of it. And the same is true with building a better body. If you didn't have to work for it, it wouldn't have anywhere near the value. And make no mistake, to "own" a healthy body for life, you will have to work hard and you will have to make sacrifices. You will have to challenge yourself, each and every day. You will have to *earn it!*

Success Story — Michele Specht

Age 28•Glendale, CA•Teacher/Actress
Increased Energy, Lost 22 lbs
Reduced Dress Size from 14 to 8

I've tried numerous "quick fixes" and "diets," but the results were limited, and when they didn't work, I felt depressed. I began Body-*for*-LIFE hoping, but not truly believing, that it would work for me. But each day I stuck with it. By the end of the first month, people were giving me compliments. By the end of the second month, comments on how bright and energetic I was becoming encouraged me to work even harder. By the end of the 12 weeks, I looked in the mirror and finally saw my true, happy self shining through!

Body-*for*-LIFE   The Power Mindset

Please write down 5 things you can do between now and this time tomorrow
that will help you move forward in the direction of your 12-week goals.

	PLAN	ACTUAL
1		
2		
3		
4		
5		

Body-*for*-LIFE   The Universal Law of Reciprocation

Please write down 2 things you can do between now and
this time tomorrow to support and encourage others.

	PLAN	ACTUAL
1		
2		

Body-*for*-LIFE   Focus on Progress, Not Perfection

Please write down 3 things you did very well today that helped
you move toward the achievement of your 12-week goals.

1	
2	
3	

Please write down one thing you will do even better tomorrow.

1	

Notes:

DAY 27

Body-*for*-LIFE — The Eating-*for*-LIFE Method™

PLAN		ACTUAL	
Meal 1		**Meal 1**	
☐ a.m. ☐ p.m.	m·	☐ a.m. ☐ p.m.	myoplex + appl
Meal 2		**Meal 2**	
☐ a.m. ☐ p.m.		☐ a.m. ☐ p.m.	myoplr
Meal 3		**Meal 3**	
☐ a.m. ☐ p.m.		☐ a.m. ☐ p.m.	troplx
Meal 4		**Meal 4**	fish
☐ a.m. ☐ p.m.		☐ a.m. ☐ p.m.	~~troplr~~ + vcs.
Meal 5		**Meal 5**	
☐ a.m. ☐ p.m.		☐ a.m. ☐ p.m.	myoplex
Meal 6		**Meal 6**	
☐ a.m. ☐ p.m.		☐ a.m. ☐ p.m.	

Notes: prn - fn 12

Body-*for*-LIFE

The 20-Minute Aerobics Solution™

Intensity Pattern	PLAN		ACTUAL	
	Planned Start Time: _____		**Actual Start Time:** _____	
	Planned End Time: _____		**Actual End Time:** _____	
	Time to Complete: 20 Minutes		**Time to Complete:** _____	

Exercise	Minute by Minute	Intensity Level	Minute by Minute	Intensity Level
	1	5	1	5
	2	5	2	6
	3	6	3	7
	4	7	4	8
recumbent	5	8	5	
pike	6	9	6	9
	7	6	7	5
	8	7	8	6
	9	8	9	
	10	9	10	7
	11	6	11	8
	12	7	12	9
	13	8	13	
	14	9	14	5
	15	6	15	6
	16	7	16	7
	17	8	17	8
High Point	18	9	18	9
	19	10	19	9
	20	5	20	5

Notes: ___3.12_____

_____HR 172 - 156_____

Bill Phillips — Lesson-*for*-LIFE

"When adversity strikes, it is vitally important to dig in your heels and not give up!"

As you begin your fifth week of the Program, chances are you've already experienced some type of unexpected adversity. (Warning: If you have not experienced adversity yet, be prepared!) Overcoming adversity, even transforming it into positive energy, is one of the most important skills you'll have the opportunity to develop during this 12-week Body-*for*-LIFE journey. When adversity strikes, whether it's a minor setback or a major obstacle, it is vitally important to dig in your heels and not give up. When times get tough, remind yourself of your reasons for accepting this Challenge. Remember that you promised yourself you would succeed, no matter what! Ask yourself, "What lesson can I learn from this experience that will make me a better person?" And ask, "How can I turn this negative into something positive?" Answer those questions, and you'll find renewed hope and determination to succeed!

Success Story — Brian Traylen

**Age 54•Marpeth, NSW, Australia•Financial Planner
Gained Muscle, Reduced Bodyfat from 14% to 8%**

Who could know in the last three weeks of my Challenge the disaster in New York and Washington would drain the time and energies of myself and my staff? With collapsing markets and client financial fears becoming all-consuming, my training looked impossible. But, from this came a greater resolve that I was going to be even more determined not to lie down and give up. By example, I gave others assurance not to quit and to continue on with life! Those last three weeks, I trained more intensely than ever, and I achieved my goals.

Body-*for*-LIFE   The Power Mindset

Please write down 5 things you can do between now and this time tomorrow
that will help you move forward in the direction of your 12-week goals.

	PLAN	ACTUAL
1		
2		
3		
4		
5		

Body-*for*-LIFE   The Universal Law of Reciprocation

Please write down 2 things you can do between now and
this time tomorrow to support and encourage others.

	PLAN	ACTUAL
1		
2		

Body-*for*-LIFE   Focus on Progress, Not Perfection

Please write down 3 things you did very well today that helped
you move toward the achievement of your 12-week goals.

1	
2	
3	

Please write down one thing you will do even better tomorrow.

1	

Notes:

Body-for-LIFE — The Eating-for-LIFE Method™

PLAN		ACTUAL	
Meal 1		**Meal 1**	
☐ a.m. ☐ p.m.	*menotech*	☐ a.m. ☐ p.m.	
Meal 2		**Meal 2**	
☐ a.m. ☐ p.m.	*trioph*	☐ a.m. ☐ p.m.	
Meal 3		**Meal 3**	
☐ a.m. ☐ p.m.	$\frac{1}{2}$ *juns*	☐ a.m. ☐ p.m.	
Meal 4		**Meal 4**	
☐ a.m. ☐ p.m.	*myoph kr*	☐ a.m. ☐ p.m.	
Meal 5		**Meal 5**	
☐ a.m. ☐ p.m.	*sclara charm fia*	☐ a.m. ☐ p.m.	
Meal 6		**Meal 6**	
☐ a.m. ☐ p.m.		☐ a.m. ☐ p.m.	

Notes:

Body-for-LIFE — Upper Body Workout

Intensity Pattern

	PLAN	ACTUAL
	Planned Start Time: 7:15	Actual Start Time: 8:20
	Planned End Time: 8:01	Actual End Time: 9:06
	Time to Complete: 46 Minutes	Time to Complete: 47'

Upper Body Muscle Groups	Exercise	Reps	Weight (lbs)	Minutes Between Sets	Intensity Level	Reps	Weight (lbs)	Minutes Between Sets	Intensity Level
Chest	inclin	12	40 lbs	1	5	12	40 lbs	1	5
	bench	10	45	1	6	10	45	1	6
	press	8	45	1	7 2:5	8	45	1	9
		6	45	1	8	6	45	1	8
High Point		12	45	0	9	12	45	0	8
		12	35	2	10	12	35	2	9
Shoulders	shoulder	12	25	1	5	12	25	1	5
	press	10	30	1	6	10	30	1	6
		8	35	1	7	8	35	1	9
		6	40	1	8	6	40	1	8
High Point		12	35	0	9	12	30	0	9
	delta rai	12	10	2	10	12	10	2	9
Back		12	40	1	5	12	12	1	5
		10	45	1	6	10	10	1	6
		8	45	1	7	8	8	1	9
		6	45	1	8	6	6	1	8
High Point		12	45	0	9	12	12	0	8
	slvn	12	30	2	10	12	12	2	9
Triceps	extens	12	25	1	5	12	25	1	5
		10	25	1	6	12		1	6
		8	25	1	7	12		1	9
		6	25	1	8	12		1	8
High Point		12	25	0	9	12	25	0	9
	dip	12	0	2	10	12	0	2	

At this point, you should be 37 minutes into your upper body workout and have 9 minutes to go.

Upper Body Muscle Groups	Exercise	Reps	Weight (lbs)	Minutes Between Sets	Intensity Level	Reps	Weight (lbs)	Minutes Between Sets	Intensity Level
Biceps	hammer	12	20	1	5	12	20	1	5
	curl	10	25	1	6	10	25	1	6
		8	25	1	7	8	25	1	9
		6	25	1	8	6	25	1	8
High Point		12	30	0	9	12	20		9
	curl	12	20	–	10	12	20 lbs		9

Notes:

Bill Phillips — Lesson-*for*-LIFE

"Finishing what you start is a habit we can all develop."

I've noticed far more people start fitness programs than finish them. Why? Quite clearly, quitting has become a *habit* for many people. The good news is we all have the potential to finish what we start, to follow through and honor self-promises. The key is to make finishing what you start a habit—a positive pattern of action. One of the things that can help is if you see every day as an example for how you'll approach the entire 12-week Program. Today, by achieving your nutrition, exercise, and mindset goals, you can feel the satisfaction of honoring self-promises and finishing what you started. Tomorrow, you have that opportunity again. And each day, as you stick with it, you'll be working to develop your ability to follow through and succeed. And that is perhaps the greatest habit you could possibly develop through this Body-*for*-LIFE experience.

Success Story — Kimberly Schaaf

Age 25•Omaha, NE•Hairstylist
Decreased Bodyfat from 17% to 10%

I was an expert at starting fitness programs but an amateur at finishing them. I kept giving up because the results were taking too long. I'm proud to say I completed Body-*for*-LIFE with more excitement than when I began. Every couple of weeks, I could see and feel the difference, and it kept me going strong. I've made this a lifestyle. I can honestly say this has been the single most satisfying self-esteem-building experience of my life. I can now look in the mirror and say I love my body and my self!

Body-*for*-LIFE The Power Mindset

Please write down 5 things you can do between now and this time tomorrow that will help you move forward in the direction of your 12-week goals.

PLAN	ACTUAL
1	
2	
3	
4	
5	

Body-*for*-LIFE The Universal Law of Reciprocation

Please write down 2 things you can do between now and this time tomorrow to support and encourage others.

PLAN	ACTUAL
1	
2	

Body-*for*-LIFE Focus on Progress, Not Perfection

Please write down 3 things you did very well today that helped you move toward the achievement of your 12-week goals.

1.
2.
3.

Please write down one thing you will do even better tomorrow.

1.

Notes:

Body-*for*-LIFE The Eating-*for*-LIFE Method™

PLAN		ACTUAL	
Meal 1		**Meal 1**	
☑a.m. ☐p.m. 7:30	microtech	☐a.m. ☐p.m.	
Meal 2		**Meal 2**	
☑a.m. ☐p.m. 10:80	½ 1~	☐a.m. ☐p.m.	
Meal 3		**Meal 3**	
☑a.m. ☐p.m. 1:0	½ 7m	☐a.m. ☐p.m.	
Meal 4		**Meal 4**	
☐a.m. ☐p.m. 4:00	Trophi ½	☐a.m. ☐p.m.	
Meal 5		**Meal 5**	
☐a.m. ☐p.m.	½ Troph	☐a.m. ☐p.m.	
Meal 6		**Meal 6**	
☐a.m. ☐p.m.	Fish rice	☐a.m. ☐p.m.	

Notes: thermodyamx
2 capsule ½ hr pre-workout

Body-*for*-LIFE

The 20-Minute Aerobics Solution™

Intensity Pattern

	PLAN		ACTUAL	
	Planned Start Time: _____		Actual Start Time: _____	
	Planned End Time: _____		Actual End Time: _____	
	Time to Complete: 20 Minutes		Time to Complete: _____	
Exercise	Minute by Minute	Intensity Level	Minute by Minute	Intensity Level
P3	1	5	1	5
	2	5	2	6
	3	6	3	7
	4	7	4	8
	5	8	5	9
	6	9	6	5
	7	6	7	6
	8	7	8	7
	9	8	9	8
	10	9	10	9
	11	6	11	
	12	7	12	5
	13	8	13	6
	14	9	14	
	15	6	15	7
	16	7	16	8
	17	8	17	9
High Point	18	9	18	9
	19	10	19	9 $\frac{1}{2}$
	20	5	20	5

Notes: 182 — 166

166 → 146

323

5.85

Bill Phillips — Lesson-*for*-LIFE

"You can restore your body to a level of health and fitness you might not have enjoyed for years."

Most people who begin the Body-*for*-LIFE Program didn't spend weeks or months falling out of shape… it's something they've been "working on" for years. Remarkably, and thankfully, it doesn't take nearly as long to rebuild the body; in fact, in as little as 12 weeks, you can restore your body to a level of health and fitness you might not have enjoyed for years. I'm often awestruck by the ability of the human body to heal, rebuild, and renew. When you decide to make a change, and then you follow a sound, scientific approach like Body-*for*-LIFE (which integrates a combination of aerobic and strength-training exercise, proper nutrition, and focused, positive thinking), you can experience a lower risk for heart disease, diabetes, and cancer. And, you can look younger, feel younger, and enjoy a higher quality of life.

Success Story — Jeff Maki

Age 38 • Seattle, WA • Engineer
Gained 15 lbs of Muscle, Lost over 50 lbs of Fat

Decades of overeating, inactivity, and obesity had finally taken a critical toll on my heart. My cardiologist's warning was blunt, "Exercise and eat right or die." Sadly, my attempts at a lifestyle tune-up disintegrated into frustration and a major case of denial. Nothing seemed to work. I hoped and prayed for a way out. I then happened to learn about Bill's Program. Hope was rekindled, and I set my goal of losing over 50 lbs of fat. And I did it! I've recaptured my future with my family and even inspired them to a healthier lifestyle!

DAY 31

Body-*for*-LIFE   The Power Mindset

Please write down 5 things you can do between now and this time tomorrow
that will help you move forward in the direction of your 12-week goals.

	PLAN	ACTUAL
1		
2		
3		
4		
5		

Body-*for*-LIFE   The Universal Law of Reciprocation

Please write down 2 things you can do between now and
this time tomorrow to support and encourage others.

	PLAN	ACTUAL
1		
2		

Body-*for*-LIFE   Focus on Progress, Not Perfection

Please write down 3 things you did very well today that helped
you move toward the achievement of your 12-week goals.

1	
2	
3	

Please write down one thing you will do even better tomorrow.

1	

Notes:

Body-*for*-LIFE   The Eating-*for*-LIFE Method™

PLAN		ACTUAL	
Meal 1		**Meal 1**	
☑ a.m. ☐ p.m. 8:03	meroזccٔ	☑ a.m. ☐ p.m. 9:70	meroזccٔ + cكرمn
Meal 2		**Meal 2**	
☐ a.m. ☑ p.m. 11:36	fۦn	☐ a.m. ☐ p.m.	
Meal 3		**Meal 3**	
☐ a.m. ☑ p.m. 2:30	myمp ٔr	☐ a.m. ☐ p.m.	
Meal 4		**Meal 4**	
☐ a.m. ☐ p.m. 9:30	myتp رۦمr	☐ a.m. ☐ p.m.	
Meal 5		**Meal 5**	
☐ a.m. ☐ p.m.	fۦٔn	☐ a.m. ☐ p.m.	
Meal 6		**Meal 6**	
☐ a.m. ☐ p.m.		☐ a.m. ☐ p.m.	

Notes: _____ p _____

Body-*for*-LIFE | Lower Body Workout

Intensity Pattern

PLAN	ACTUAL
Planned Start Time: 7:30	Actual Start Time: _____
Planned End Time: 8:12	Actual End Time: _____
Time to Complete: 42 Minutes	Time to Complete: _____

Lower Body Muscle Groups	Exercise	Reps	Weight (lbs)	Minutes Between Sets	Intensity Level	Reps	Weight (lbs)	Minutes Between Sets	Intensity Level
Quads	extn	12	120	1	5	12	120	1	5
		10	125	1	6	10	125	1	6
		8		1	7 2:31	8	125	1	7
		6		1	8 4:13	6	125	1	8
High Point	squat	12		0	9 5.54	12	125	0	9
		12	90	2	10	12	90	2	
Hamstrings	-curl	12	65	1	5	12	65	1	5
		10	70	1	6 11 6	10	70	1	6
		8	75	1	7 13 8	8	75	1	7
		6	80	1	8 15 2	6	75→60	1	8
High Point	-lunge	12	75	0	9 17.7	12	60	0	9
		12	85	2	10	12	35	2	9
Calves	ex	12	40	1	5 22.5	12	40	1	5
		10	45	1	6 23.1	10	45	1	6
		8	45	1	7 26.09	8	45	1	7
		6	45	1	8 27.2	6	45	1	8
High Point		12	45	0	9 28.47	12	45	0	9
		12	40	2	10	12	40	2	9

At this point, you should be 31 minutes into your lower body workout and have 11 minutes to go.

Lower Body Muscle Groups	Exercise	Reps	Weight (lbs)	Minutes Between Sets	Intensity Level	Reps	Weight (lbs)	Minutes Between Sets	Intensity Level
Abs	DCN reverse	12	12	1	5	12	Ø	1	5
		10	10	1	6	10	Ø	1	6
	crunch	8	8	1	7 35.73	8	Ø	1	7
		6	6	1	8 37.15	6	Ø	1	8
High Point		12	12	0	9 38.5	12	Ø	0	8
	prone	12	13	-	10	12	Ø	2	9

Notes: curls go down to (60)
Next

Bill Phillips — Lesson-*for*-LIFE

"It's what you do most of the time, not some of the time, that shapes you."

Today I want to share something that I would like you to keep in mind: No one is perfect. We all make mistakes. Therefore, no one can follow the Body-*for*-LIFE Program "perfectly." Even I miss workouts and meals from time to time, and even my plans sometimes get interrupted by traffic jams, delayed airline flights, meetings that take longer than expected, and even over-sleeping. But those things are the exception, not the rule. Most of the time, I eat six nutritious protein- and carbohydrate-balanced meals a day. Most of the time, I exercise intensely, first thing in the morning. Most of the time, I keep a positive mindset and am optimistic. And most of the time, I feel healthy and energetic. Remember, it's what we do *most* of the time that shapes us, not what we do some of the time. So, don't worry if you're not "perfect."

Success Story — Robyn Seeber

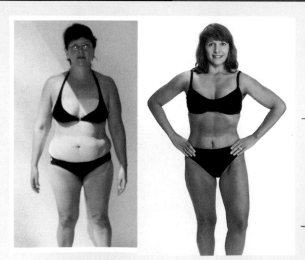

Age 46•Webster, NY•Program Manager
Reduced Bodyfat from 29% to 19%
Lost 19 lbs of Fat, Gained Strength

After I read Body-*for*-LIFE, I thought it made complete sense and decided to try it. I set specific written goals. I knew where I was going and why. I knew what I needed to change. Life as a working mother is a delicate balancing act, and I had to improve my family's daily schedule to incorporate my work-outs. I hadn't been taking any time for me. I now view myself differently and know that others do too. I'm *not* perfect, but I feel wonderful, energetic, and positive for the first time in years. And I feel the best is yet to come!

Body-*for*-LIFE | The Power Mindset

Please write down 5 things you can do between now and this time tomorrow
that will help you move forward in the direction of your 12-week goals.

	PLAN	ACTUAL
1		
2		
3		
4		
5		

Body-*for*-LIFE | The Universal Law of Reciprocation

Please write down 2 things you can do between now and
this time tomorrow to support and encourage others.

	PLAN	ACTUAL
1		
2		

Body-*for*-LIFE | Focus on Progress, Not Perfection

Please write down 3 things you did very well today that helped
you move toward the achievement of your 12-week goals.

1	
2	
3	

Please write down one thing you will do even better tomorrow.

1	

Notes:

Body-*for*-LIFE   The Eating-*for*-LIFE Method™

PLAN		ACTUAL	
Meal 1		**Meal 1**	
☑ a.m. ☐ p.m.	~~protein~~ myoplx	☐ a.m. ☐ p.m.	
Meal 2		**Meal 2**	
☐ a.m. ☐ p.m.	$\frac{1}{2}$ trioplex	☐ a.m. ☐ p.m.	
Meal 3		**Meal 3**	
☐ a.m. ☐ p.m.	$\frac{1}{2}$ tuna	☐ a.m. ☐ p.m.	
Meal 4		**Meal 4**	
☐ a.m. ☐ p.m.	myoplx	☐ a.m. ☐ p.m.	
Meal 5		**Meal 5**	
☐ a.m. ☐ p.m.	fish/chkn salad	☐ a.m. ☐ p.m.	
Meal 6		**Meal 6**	
☐ a.m. ☐ p.m.	merocco	☐ a.m. ☐ p.m.	

Notes:

Body-for-LIFE

The 20-Minute Aerobics Solution™

Intensity Pattern

	PLAN		ACTUAL	
	Planned Start Time: 7;00		Actual Start Time: 8:01	
	Planned End Time: 7:2.		Actual End Time: 625	
	Time to Complete: 20 Minutes		Time to Complete: 2.	
Exercise	Minute by Minute	Intensity Level	Minute by Minute	Intensity Level
	1	5	1	5
	2	5	2	
	3	6	3	6
	4	7	4	7
P3 recumbent	5	8	5	8
	6	9	6	9
	7	6	7	
	8	7	8	5
	9	8	9	6
	10	9	10	7
	11	6	11	8
	12	7	12	9
	13	8	13	5
	14	9	14	6
	15	6	15	7
	16	7	16	8
	17	8	17	
High Point	18	9	18	9
High Point	19	10	19	9
	20	5	20	5

Notes: 178 → 156
        19   20

Bill Phillips — Lesson-*for*-LIFE

"Forgiveness is a priceless gift you can give for free."

One of the things I've noticed about people in general is that they're too darned hard on themselves. I see so many good people who don't even know how good they are. They carry bags of guilt, filled to the brim, with them day and night, expending precious energy. That "baggage," like pounds of unhealthy bodyfat, needs to be shed in order to move upward and onward. The process of breaking free involves forgiving. Forgiving others, and most important, *forgiving yourself*. Perhaps you haven't cared for your body the way you feel you could have or should have. Perhaps you've broken self-promises. Perhaps you've let yourself down. If so, you're not alone. Virtually everyone has felt like that at some point. But you don't have to let that stop you. The key is to forgive and vow to try harder and do better in the future. Drop that baggage and move on!

Success Story — Charles DeConnick

Age 36 • Birkenhead, New Zealand
Reduced Bodyfat from 24% to 9%

I needed something to lift me out of a slump. I was tired, mentally and physically. I felt ashamed and wanted a better life. I decided to try Body-*for*-LIFE. My before and after photos show my physical transformation after 12 weeks, but more than that, I now have a seemingly endless reserve of energy, and each and every day, I feel great and enjoy life more than ever! I am no longer in a slump or a rut; I now have bigger goals in life. And I am able to tackle those goals with renewed zest because of my increased energy!

Body-*for*-LIFE The Power Mindset

Please write down 5 things you can do between now and this time tomorrow that will help you move forward in the direction of your 12-week goals.

	PLAN	ACTUAL
1		
2		
3		
4		
5		

Body-*for*-LIFE The Universal Law of Reciprocation

Please write down 2 things you can do between now and this time tomorrow to support and encourage others.

	PLAN	ACTUAL
1		
2		

Body-*for*-LIFE Focus on Progress, Not Perfection

Please write down 3 things you did very well today that helped you move toward the achievement of your 12-week goals.

1	
2	
3	

Please write down one thing you will do even better tomorrow.

1	

Notes:

Body-for-LIFE The Eating-for-LIFE Method™

PLAN		ACTUAL	
Meal 1		**Meal 1**	
☐ a.m. ☐ p.m.	mesorech ~~apple~~	☑ a.m. ☐ p.m.	meded
Meal 2		**Meal 2**	
☐ a.m. ☐ p.m.	myopia	☐ a.m. ☐ p.m.	
Meal 3		**Meal 3**	
☐ a.m. ☐ p.m.	troplex	☐ a.m. ☐ p.m.	
Meal 4		**Meal 4**	
☐ a.m. ☐ p.m.	Triuple	☐ a.m. ☐ p.m.	
Meal 5		**Meal 5**	
☐ a.m. ☐ p.m.	fish + salad	☐ a.m. ☐ p.m.	
Meal 6		**Meal 6**	
☐ a.m. ☐ p.m.		☐ a.m. ☐ p.m.	

Notes: Xenaar ~~ev~~ (2)

Body-*for*-LIFE Upper Body Workout

Intensity Pattern

	PLAN		ACTUAL
Planned Start Time: 7:00			Actual Start Time: 7:10
Planned End Time: 7:46			Actual End Time: 7:53
Time to Complete: 46 Minutes			Time to Complete: 43

Upper Body Muscle Groups	Exercise	Reps	Weight (lbs)	Minutes Between Sets	Intensity Level	Reps	Weight (lbs)	Minutes Between Sets	Intensity Level
Chest	incln	12	40	1	5	12	40	1	8
	avapul	10	45	1	6	10	45	1	6
	pru	8	45	1	7	8 2.5'	45	1	7
		6	45	1	8	6 3.5'	45	1	8
High Point		12	45	0	9	12	65-40'	0	9
	Fly.	12	35	2	10	12	35-30	2	10
Shoulders		12	20	1	5	12	20	1	5
		10	25	1	6 11	10	25	1	6
		8	30	1	7	8	30	1	7
		6	35	1	8 14,3'	6	35	1	1
High Point		12	30	0	9 15.5	12	30	6	9
		12	10	2	10	12	10	2	9
Back	rows	12	40	1	5 20	12	30	1	5
		10	45	1	6	10	40	1	6
		8	45	1	7 2:	8	45	1	7
		6	45	1	8 23 R	6	45	1	8
High Point		12	45	0	9	12	45	6	8
		12	30	2	10	12	25	2	9
Triceps	ext	12	25	1	5 27	12	25	1	5
		10		1	6	12		1	6
		8		1	7	12		1	7
		6		1	8	12		1	Y
High Point		12		0	9	12	12	0	3
	dips	12		2	10		12	2	

At this point, you should be 37 minutes into your upper body workout and have 9 minutes to go.

Biceps		12	20	1	5	12	20	1	5
		10	25	1	6 37 3	10	25	1	6
		8	30	1	7 38	8	30	1	9
		6	35	1	8	6	31	1	8
High Point		12	30	0	9 40.	12	30	0	3
		12	25	–	10	12		2	

Notes:

Bill Phillips — Lesson-*for*-LIFE

"It's hard to do the right thing in the wrong situation."

By far and away, the most challenging aspect of this Program, for me, is eating right. What about you? For me, the workouts are no problem. I actually enjoy them, especially the weightlifting. However, eating right is a challenge. And for over 15 years it's been that way. One of the things I've learned is that it's hard for me to do the right thing in the wrong situation. For example, if my kitchen is stocked with cookies, candies, ice cream, chips, etc., odds are I'll tear into it, usually in the late evening when "eating wrong" does the most damage. So what I do is make sure my kitchen is not a trap but rather a treasure chest of good nutrition, stocked with fresh fruits and vegetables, eggs, chicken, fish, yogurt, cottage cheese, brown rice, potatoes, Myoplex™ nutrition shakes, and lots of bottled water. That's the right situation for me.

Success Story — Shana Ruggiero

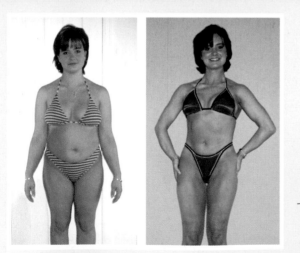

Age 23 • Colorado Springs, CO
Reduced Bodyfat from 27% to 14%
Gained 8 lbs of Muscle, Lost 22 lbs of Fat

I tried the uneducated way of losing weight... STARVATION. Yes, I began losing scale weight by the pounds, but I had no energy and was grumpy, and I was always hungry. I quit the starvation diet and gained all the weight I'd lost and more. I just wasn't eating right. I didn't have the energy to go out, and my clothes didn't fit anymore. Then I tried Bill's Program. Each week, my energy went up and my bodyfat went down. Now I know how to feed my body. I eat often and I enjoy healthy foods. And I feel wonderful!

Body-*for*-LIFE The Power Mindset

Please write down 5 things you can do between now and this time tomorrow that will help you move forward in the direction of your 12-week goals.

	PLAN	ACTUAL
1		
2		
3		
4		
5		

Body-*for*-LIFE The Universal Law of Reciprocation

Please write down 2 things you can do between now and this time tomorrow to support and encourage others.

	PLAN	ACTUAL
1		
2		

Body-*for*-LIFE Focus on Progress, Not Perfection

Please write down 3 things you did very well today that helped you move toward the achievement of your 12-week goals.

1	
2	
3	

Please write down one thing you will do even better tomorrow.

1	

Notes:

Body-*for*-LIFE   The Eating-*for*-LIFE Method™

PLAN		ACTUAL	
Meal 1		**Meal 1**	
☐ a.m. ☐ p.m.	menrcer	☐ a.m. ☐ p.m.	
Meal 2		**Meal 2**	
☐ a.m. ☐ p.m.	myoplex tuns	☐ a.m. ☐ p.m.	
Meal 3		**Meal 3**	
☐ a.m. ☐ p.m.	Trioplex + myoplex	☐ a.m. ☐ p.m.	
Meal 4		**Meal 4**	
☐ a.m. ☐ p.m.	trioplex + 2	☐ a.m. ☐ p.m.	
Meal 5		**Meal 5**	
☐ a.m. ☐ p.m.	trioplex chicas	☐ a.m. ☐ p.m.	
Meal 6		**Meal 6**	
☐ a.m. ☐ p.m.	chicn salad	☐ a.m. ☐ p.m.	

Notes:

DAY 34

Body-*for*-LIFE

The 20-Minute Aerobics Solution™

Intensity Pattern	PLAN		ACTUAL	
	Planned Start Time: 6:65		Actual Start Time: ___	
	Planned End Time: 6:25		Actual End Time: ___	
	Time to Complete: 20 Minutes		Time to Complete: ___	
Exercise	Minute by Minute	Intensity Level	Minute by Minute	Intensity Level
P₃ recumpe(?)	1	5	1	5
	2	5	2	6
	3	6	3	7
	4	7	4	8
	5	8	5	
	6	9	6	9
	7	6	7	5
	8	7	8	6
	9	8	9	7
	10	9	10	
	11	6	11	8
	12	7	12	9
	13	8	13	5
	14	9	14	6
	15	6	15	7
	16	7	16	8
	17	8	17	9
High Point	18	9	18	10
	19	10	19	
	20	5	20	5

Notes: ¹⁹ 176 — ²⁰ 160

866(?)

Bill Phillips — Lesson-*for*-LIFE

"You have to want to change more than you want to stay the same."

One of the interesting contradictions of life is that we want to change, and yet at some level, we want to stay the same. But you can't do both. Clearly, you can't be a before photo and an after photo at the same time. Every single one of the success stories you'll read about in this book was created, to a significant degree, by the person *wanting to change* more than they wanted to stay the same. Sometimes people were absolutely at the end of their ropes—their health failing, their relationships suffering, their lives falling apart. Other times, people wanted to change because they knew that their lives could be even better. Whatever your reasons are for wanting to change, please don't lose sight of them! Remind yourself of your reasons daily and allow them to help keep you going strong.

Success Story — Ray Wiest

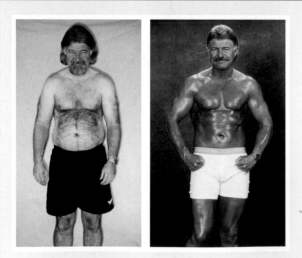

Age 47 • Roseville, CA • Deputy Sheriff
Lost 30 lbs of Fat, Reduced Waist from 35" to 32"
Reduced Cholesterol Level from 230 to 162

With a family history of heart disease, my life literally depended on improving my health, so I dedicated this effort to my family. The greatest obstacle for me to overcome was "myself." I have lived a lifetime of allowing my excuses to get the best of me. I realized that ultimately I am the one who controls the successes and failures in my life. As the inches and pounds melted away, that reflection in the mirror allowed me to believe in "me." I learned that nothing drives success as effectively as success itself.

Body-*for*-LIFE The Power Mindset

Please write down 5 things you can do between now and this time tomorrow
that will help you move forward in the direction of your 12-week goals.

	PLAN	ACTUAL
1		
2		
3		
4		
5		

Body-*for*-LIFE The Universal Law of Reciprocation

Please write down 2 things you can do between now and
this time tomorrow to support and encourage others.

	PLAN	ACTUAL
1		
2		

Body-*for*-LIFE Focus on Progress, Not Perfection

Please write down 3 things you did very well today that helped
you move toward the achievement of your 12-week goals.

1	
2	
3	

Please write down one thing you will do even better tomorrow.

1	

Notes:

Body-for-LIFE — The Eating-for-LIFE Method™

PLAN		ACTUAL	
Meal 1		**Meal 1**	
☐ a.m. ☐ p.m.	mesozccn shum	☐ a.m. ☐ p.m.	myopta
Meal 2		**Meal 2**	
☐ a.m. ☐ p.m.	lvich	☐ a.m. ☐ p.m.	lcmp s rulu9
Meal 3		**Meal 3**	
☐ a.m. ☐ p.m.	Trioplx	☐ a.m. ☐ p.m.	myopn
Meal 4		**Meal 4**	
☐ a.m. ☐ p.m.	myoplcx	☐ a.m. ☐ p.m.	7 ivpn
Meal 5		**Meal 5**	
☐ a.m. ☐ p.m.	chicn	☐ a.m. ☐ p.m.	cnin ttaboull,
Meal 6		**Meal 6**	
☐ a.m. ☐ p.m.		☐ a.m. ☐ p.m.	

Notes:

Body-*for*-LIFE Lower Body Workout

Intensity Pattern		PLAN				ACTUAL			
		Planned Start Time: 6:15				Actual Start Time: 8:98			
		Planned End Time: 6:49				Actual End Time: 5:30			
		Time to Complete: 42 Minutes				Time to Complete: 42:			

Lower Body Muscle Groups	Exercise	Reps	Weight (lbs)	Minutes Between Sets	Intensity Level	Reps	Weight (lbs)	Minutes Between Sets	Intensity Level
Quads	ext	12	120	1 40'	5	12	120	40'	5
		10	125	1	6	10	125		6
		8		1	7 1.52	8	125		7
		6		1	8 3.	6	125		8
High Point	squat	12		0	9 4.3	12	125	0	8
		12	90	2	10	12	90	2	
Hamstrings	curl	12	65	1	5	12	65	1	5
		10	70	1	6	10	70	1	7
		8	75	1	7 11.23	8	75	2+9	8
		6	80	1	8 13-0	6	75	1	9
High Point	leg	12	75	0	9 152	12	75-6 85 5-10 1		9
		12	35	2	10	12	35		9
Calves	ext	12	40	1	5	12	40		5
	on jn'	10	45	1	6	10	45		6
		8		1	7	8	45		7
		6		1	8	6	45		8
High Point	dvo,t	12		0	9	12	45		8
		12	45	2	10	12	45		9

At this point, you should be 31 minutes into your lower body workout and have 11 minutes to go.

Abs	revers	12		1	5	12			5
	cnnit	10		1	6	10			6
		8		1	7	8			7
		6		1	8	6			8
High Point	pull sann	12		0	9	12	12		8
		12		-	10	12	12		9

Notes: curls — too much weight
arp o 7 5 lb

Bill Phillips   Lesson-*for*-LIFE

"How you feed your body today will determine the productiveness of yesterday's intense exercise session."

By this point in the Program, I don't need to convince you that your intense workouts are having an effect on your body. You've felt the muscles burn while you're exercising, and, no doubt, you've experienced the muscle fatigue and soreness (both of which are natural and part of the transformation process). With that in mind, I'd like to ask you to give special attention to how you're eating today. Remember, we must feed our bodies properly to replenish vitamins, minerals, protein, essential fatty acids, and other nutrients. At this very moment, your muscles are undergoing a "remodeling" process. They're repairing damage from yesterday's workout, and they are pulling the amino acids and other nutrients needed for repair and recovery from what is circulating in your bloodstream *right now*. Please consider that how you feed your body today will, to a significant extent, determine the productiveness of yesterday's intense exercise session.

Success Story   Allen Bieber

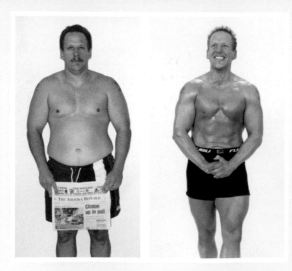

Age 40 • Tucson, AZ • Air Traffic Controller
Improved Health, Decreased Bodyfat by 27%

Thirteen years ago, I was a Marine in the best shape of my life. Then I quit working out. Combined with my poor eating habits, the weight started piling on. I could barely find clothes that would fit. My son introduced me to Body-*for*-LIFE and encouraged me to try this Program. I joined a gym, ate six meals a day, and trained intensely. And it worked. This experience changed my life. I no longer face the pain and despair of being obese. I hope my success will show people that the chains of obesity can be broken.

Body-*for*-LIFE   The Power Mindset

Please write down 5 things you can do between now and this time tomorrow that will help you move forward in the direction of your 12-week goals.

	PLAN	ACTUAL
1		
2		
3		
4		
5		

Body-*for*-LIFE   The Universal Law of Reciprocation

Please write down 2 things you can do between now and this time tomorrow to support and encourage others.

	PLAN	ACTUAL
1		
2		

Body-*for*-LIFE   Focus on Progress, Not Perfection

Please write down 3 things you did very well today that helped you move toward the achievement of your 12-week goals.

1	
2	
3	

Please write down one thing you will do even better tomorrow.

1	

Notes:

Body-*for*-LIFE The Eating-*for*-LIFE Method™

PLAN		ACTUAL	
Meal 1		**Meal 1**	
☐ a.m. ☐ p.m.	menica	☐ a.m. ☐ p.m.	
Meal 2		**Meal 2**	
☐ a.m. ☐ p.m.	myopka	☐ a.m. ☐ p.m.	
Meal 3		**Meal 3**	
☐ a.m. ☐ p.m.	triopka	☐ a.m. ☐ p.m.	
Meal 4		**Meal 4**	
☐ a.m. ☐ p.m.	myopka	☐ a.m. ☐ p.m.	
Meal 5		**Meal 5**	
☐ a.m. ☐ p.m.	fun salad	☐ a.m. ☐ p.m.	
Meal 6		**Meal 6**	
☐ a.m. ☐ p.m.	protin shak	☐ a.m. ☐ p.m.	

Notes:

Body-*for*-LIFE

The 20-Minute Aerobics Solution™

Intensity Pattern

	PLAN		ACTUAL	
	Planned Start Time: 7:15		Actual Start Time: 8:15	
	Planned End Time: 7:35		Actual End Time: 8:31	
	Time to Complete: 20 Minutes		Time to Complete: _____	
Exercise	Minute by Minute	Intensity Level	Minute by Minute	Intensity Level
	1	5	1	5
	2	5	2	6
	3	6	3	7
	4	7	4	
	5	8	5	8
	6	9	6	9
ρ 3	7	6	7	
	8	7	8	5
	9	8	9	6
	10	9	10	7
	11	6	11	8
	12	7	12	9
	13	8	13	5
	14	9	14	6
	15	6	15	7
	16	7	16	8
	17	8	17	
High Point	18	9	18	9
	19	10	19	8
	20	5	20	5

Notes: ____ HA (192) _____

_____

Bill Phillips — Lesson-*for*-LIFE

"Intensity means giving it all you've got, and more!"

"How do I know if I'm training with the proper amount of intensity?" That's one of the questions I'm frequently asked. My answer: "Are you *really*, truly giving every last bit of energy and effort on your high point sets, *and then some?!* Are you concentrating all your energy and breaking through your perceived level of 'maximum effort'?" I don't know the answers to those questions: only you do. If you're not giving your absolute best, *and then some*, don't expect maximum results. To achieve a breakthrough transformation, you have to have breakthroughs in your training intensity every week. So today, test yourself... Think about hitting your high points with more intensity than ever! Imagine me standing there during your high point sets, asking you, "Is that your absolute best effort? If so, *give me even one more rep!*"

Success Story — Gino and Tami DePalma

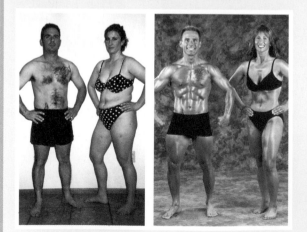

Ages 33 and 32•Arvada, CO
Police Officer / PR Firm Owner
Gino Reduced Bodyfat from 11% to 5%
Tami Decreased Dress Size from 12 to 6

We were as dedicated to this Program as we are to our wedding vows. Watching each other succeed built a bond and fostered deep respect for each other. This is among the most constructive things we've done for each other, our marriage, and ourselves. Now that we're focused, nothing stops us. Intense workouts are the key for us. After that, everything else falls into place. We've also developed the skill to accept ourselves as we improve and even congratulate ourselves on our weekly progress.

Body-*for*-LIFE The Power Mindset

Please write down 5 things you can do between now and this time tomorrow that will help you move forward in the direction of your 12-week goals.

	PLAN	ACTUAL
1		
2		
3		
4		
5		

Body-*for*-LIFE The Universal Law of Reciprocation

Please write down 2 things you can do between now and this time tomorrow to support and encourage others.

	PLAN	ACTUAL
1		
2		

Body-*for*-LIFE Focus on Progress, Not Perfection

Please write down 3 things you did very well today that helped you move toward the achievement of your 12-week goals.

1	
2	
3	

Please write down one thing you will do even better tomorrow.

1	

Notes:

Body-*for*-LIFE   The Eating-*for*-LIFE Method™

PLAN		ACTUAL	
Meal 1		**Meal 1**	
☑ a.m. ☐ p.m. ♯.B		☐ a.m. ☐ p.m.	
Meal 2		**Meal 2**	
☑ a.m. ☐ p.m.	½ Tuna	☐ a.m. ☐ p.m.	
Meal 3		**Meal 3**	
☐ a.m. ☑ p.m. 1.w	CALD + sclw	☐ a.m. ☐ p.m.	
Meal 4		**Meal 4**	
☐ a.m. ☐ p.m. 4	½ 1 crips	☐ a.m. ☐ p.m.	
Meal 5		**Meal 5**	
☐ a.m. ☐ p.m. 4		☐ a.m. ☐ p.m.	
Meal 6		**Meal 6**	
☐ a.m. ☐ p.m.		☐ a.m. ☐ p.m.	

Notes: _____ xcnuar sv·n _____

Body-*for*-LIFE — Upper Body Workout

Intensity Pattern

	PLAN	ACTUAL
Planned Start Time: _____		Actual Start Time: _____
Planned End Time: _____		Actual End Time: _____
Time to Complete: 46 Minutes		Time to Complete: _____

Upper Body Muscle Groups	Exercise	Reps	Weight (lbs)	Minutes Between Sets	Intensity Level	Reps	Weight (lbs)	Minutes Between Sets	Intensity Level
Chest	piesio	12	50	1	5	12	40	1	5
	good	10	45	1	6	10	45	1	6
	ex	8	45	1	7	8	45	1	7
		6	45	1	8	6	45	1	8
High Point	fly	12	45	0	9	12	45	0	9
		12	90	2	10	12	30	2	9
Shoulders	military	12	28	1	5	12	28	1	5
	press	10	36	1	6	10	36	1	6
		8	35	1	7	8	35	1	7
		6	40	1	8	6	40	1	8
High Point		12	35	0	9	12	35	0	8
	rear	12	10	2	10	12	10	2	9
Back	row	12	40	1	5	12	40	1	5
		10	45	1	6	10	45	1	6
		8	45	1	7	8	45	1	7
		6	45	1	8	6	45	1	8
High Point		12	45	0	9	12	45	0	9
	shrug	12	25	2	10	12	30	2	9
Triceps	ex	12	25	1	5	12	25	1	5
		10		1	6	10	25	1	6
		8		1	7	8	25	1	7
		6		1	8	6	25	1	8
High Point		12		0	9	12	25	0	7
	chip	12	0	2	10	12	0	2	5

At this point, you should be 37 minutes into your upper body workout and have 9 minutes to go.

Biceps	hemmer	12	20	1	5	20	12	1	5
	curl	10	25	1	6	25	10	1	6
		8	0	1	7	30	8	1	7
		6	35	1	8	35	6	1	8
High Point		12	30	0	9	30		0	
	curl	12	30	–	10	25		2	

Notes:

_____

_____

Bill Phillips   Lesson-*for*-LIFE

"The only way to truly fail
is to quit trying."

I was at a book signing at a Barnes & Noble store in Wichita, Kansas. A healthy, 34-year-old woman named Kimberly introduced herself. Somewhat sullen, she asked if I could write some encouraging words in her book, explaining that she's tried several times to complete the 12-week Program but had "failed" each time. "Failed?!" I replied. "You look wonderful!" She explained that through her efforts, she'd lost 15 lbs of bodyfat and increased her muscle definition and energy. But she again explained that she "failed" because each time she tried to complete the 12-week Program, something would come up, and she would fall off track. What I explained to Kimberly, and what I want to share with you, is that as long as you keep trying, you will *never* fail. Also, give yourself credit where credit is due—celebrate any and all progress!

Success Story   Pamela Hickerson

Age 47•Malibu, CA•Sales and Marketing
Lost 22 lbs of Fat, Gained 2 lbs of Muscle
Decreased Dress Size from 11/12 to 5/6

After turning 47, I felt no energy, no muscle tone, no spark. I needed a new challenge. I decided to give it all I had and not let anything get in my way of becoming a success story! I was rarely able to complete anything I started, but I gained an inner sense of strength and confidence by completing this. I learned how to set goals and honor my self-promises to achieve them. This new energetic and positive attitude has enabled me to overcome fears and turn adversity into something positive!

Body-*for*-LIFE   The Power Mindset

Please write down 5 things you can do between now and this time tomorrow
that will help you move forward in the direction of your 12-week goals.

PLAN	ACTUAL
1	
2	
3	
4	
5	

Body-*for*-LIFE   The Universal Law of Reciprocation

Please write down 2 things you can do between now and
this time tomorrow to support and encourage others.

PLAN	ACTUAL
1	
2	

Body-*for*-LIFE   Focus on Progress, Not Perfection

Please write down 3 things you did very well today that helped
you move toward the achievement of your 12-week goals.

1	
2	
3	

Please write down one thing you will do even better tomorrow.

1	

Notes:

DAY 39

Body-*for*-LIFE | The Eating-*for*-LIFE Method™

PLAN		ACTUAL	

Meal 1

PLAN
☐ a.m.
☐ p.m. mentcy

ACTUAL
☑ a.m.
☐ p.m. myuphs
10:00 ↑ apth

Meal 2

PLAN
☐ a.m.
☐ p.m. trioph
½ 1

ACTUAL
☐ a.m.
☐ p.m.

9:30 trioplex

Meal 3

PLAN
☐ a.m.
☐ p.m.

ACTUAL
☐ a.m. +
☐ p.m.

Meal 4

PLAN
☐ a.m.
☐ p.m.

ACTUAL
5:00 ☐ a.m. messtcly
☐ p.m.

Meal 5

PLAN
☐ a.m. fih
☐ p.m. tralve

ACTUAL
8:00 ☐ a.m. trocy
☐ p.m. 1 rcy
trll

Meal 6

PLAN
☐ a.m. poti
☐ p.m.

ACTUAL
11:30 ☑ a.m. ½ trioph
☐ p.m.

Notes:

Body-*for*-LIFE | The 20-Minute Aerobics Solution™

Intensity Pattern	PLAN		ACTUAL	
	Planned Start Time: 6:3°		Actual Start Time: 8:3ᴶ	
	Planned End Time: 6:5°		Actual End Time: 8:5ᴶ	
	Time to Complete: 20 Minutes		Time to Complete: 2°	

Exercise	Minute by Minute	Intensity Level	Minute by Minute	Intensity Level
ß3 recumbian Dike level 3	1	5	1	5
	2	5	2	6
	3	6	3	7
	4	7	4	8
	5	8	5	9
	6	9	6	5
	7	6	7	6
	8	7	8	7
	9	8	9	8
	10	9	10	9
	11	6	11	5
	12	7	12	6
	13	8	13	7
	14	9	14	8
	15	6	15	9
	16	7	16	10
	17	8	17	
High Point	18	9	18	
	19	10	19	
	20	5	20	

Notes: S. 6ᴶ N   ᴴR ⟨182⟩
         ⟨3+3 Cd⟩   ⟨170⟩

Bill Phillips   Lesson-*for*-LIFE

"If you miss a workout, you miss it. Put it behind you and move on!"

By this point in the Program, nine out of ten people will have missed a workout… or two. In fact, the vast majority of people whose before and after pictures and success stories are featured in this book missed a few workouts during the course of the 12-week Program. And still, as you can clearly see, they succeeded anyway. The key is sticking with it, day after day, and finishing all 12 weeks. My advice is that if you miss a workout, *don't* try to make up for it by doubling up the next day. For example, if you missed yesterday's aerobic workout, don't try to "make up for it" by doing your leg training *and* aerobics today. That approach can put you in a "reactive" mode rather than a "proactive" position where you are in control. So if you miss a workout, you miss it. Put it behind you. Vow to try harder in the future, plan better, and move forward!

Success Story   Brad Wadlow

**Age 30•Desloge, MO•Drilling Rig Operator
Gained 20 lbs of Muscle, Lost 22 lbs of Fat**

I've learned that you sometimes get what you want, and other times you don't. But if you never even try to do something great, you have already lost. Those who have the guts to give it their best are already winners. I think this is such an important thing for people to realize. Try and try again and you may very well become a bigger success than you imagined. That's what happened to me. This is a new way of life for me. I now have a stronger body, higher self-esteem, and a purpose in life.

Body-*for*-LIFE   The Power Mindset

Please write down 5 things you can do between now and this time tomorrow
that will help you move forward in the direction of your 12-week goals.

	PLAN	ACTUAL
1		
2		
3		
4		
5		

Body-*for*-LIFE   The Universal Law of Reciprocation

Please write down 2 things you can do between now and
this time tomorrow to support and encourage others.

	PLAN	ACTUAL
1		
2		

Body-*for*-LIFE   Focus on Progress, Not Perfection

Please write down 3 things you did very well today that helped
you move toward the achievement of your 12-week goals.

1	
2	
3	

Please write down one thing you will do even better tomorrow.

1	

Notes:

DAY 40

Body-*for*-LIFE   The Eating-*for*-LIFE Method™

PLAN		ACTUAL	
Meal 1		**Meal 1**	
☐ a.m. ☐ p.m.	meavu	☐ a.m. ☐ p.m.	trioplea F-11 P~ 12
Meal 2		**Meal 2**	
☐ a.m. ☐ p.m.	vom rsprh	☐ a.m. ☐ p.m.	salmon ves 1'1
Meal 3		**Meal 3**	
☐ a.m. ☐ p.m.	sclmm	☐ a.m. ☐ p.m.	myopler
Meal 4		**Meal 4**	
☐ a.m. ☐ p.m.	myopli	☐ a.m. ☐ p.m.	sclmon + chich
Meal 5		**Meal 5**	
☐ a.m. ☐ p.m.	sclmm	☐ a.m. ☐ p.m.	
Meal 6		**Meal 6**	
☐ a.m. ☐ p.m.	mervxch	☐ a.m. ☐ p.m.	

Notes:

Body-*for*-LIFE

Lower Body Workout

Intensity Pattern

	PLAN	ACTUAL
Planned Start Time: 6:15		Actual Start Time: 6:33
Planned End Time: 6:41		Actual End Time: ___
Time to Complete: 42 Minutes		Time to Complete: 33

Lower Body Muscle Groups	Exercise	Reps	Weight (lbs)	Minutes Between Sets	Intensity Level	Reps	Weight (lbs)	Minutes Between Sets	Intensity Level
Quads	2x7	12	120	1	5	12	120	1	5
		10	125	1	6	10	125	1	6
		8	125	1	7 2:49	8	125	1	7
		6	125	1	8 4:21	6	125	1	8
High Point	sqr	12	125	0	9 5:51	12	125	0	8
		12	90	2	10	12	90	2	8
Hamstrings	curl	12	60	1	5 8:37	12	60	1	5
		10	65	1	6 11:15	10	65	1	6
		8	90	1	7 12:51	8	70 2	1	7
		6	75	1	8 14:36	6	75 4	1	8
High Point		12	70	0	9 16:24	12	70	0	5
		12	35	2	10	12	35	2	3
Calves	ex	12	40	1	5 22:6	12	4,0	1	5
		10	45	1	6 24:3	10	45	1	6
		8	45	1	7 25:0	8	45	1	7
		6	45	1	8 26:5	6	45	1	8
High Point	curl -9	12	45	0	9 28:13	12	45	0	
		12	45	2	10	12	45	2	
At this point, you should be 31 minutes into your lower body workout and have 11 minutes to go.									
Abs	reverse curl	12	12	1	5 30:33	12	0	1	5
		10	10	1	6	10	8	1	6
		8	8	1	7 34:50	8	9	1	7
		6	6	1	8	6	8	1	8
High Point		12	12	0	9	12	12	0	3
	reverse	12	12	-	10	12	12	-	3

Notes:

Bill Phillips   Lesson-*for*-LIFE

"Take this Program seriously, but have fun!"

Make no mistake, improving your health, transforming your body, and lifting yourself to a higher quality of life is serious stuff! Yet, it can and should become *fun*. Everything—from setting and achieving your daily goals to planning, preparing, and consuming healthy, nutritious meals—can and should become enjoyable. Yes, I know that throughout this Program you may have to face aspects of your life and your *self* that you don't really like, that don't reflect the *real* you, but still, you can feel good about the fact you are making a change for the better. Imagine the pride, the satisfaction, the positive energy you'll have when you take your after photo and tell your success story! Imagine now what you will feel like *then*. And realize you're doing this work to enjoy your life more—to have more fun with this gift of life we've all been given!

Success Story   "Judy" Yumiko McCollor

Age 40•Kihei, HI•Wife/Mother
Reduced Bodyfat from 21% to 14%
Decreased from Size 6 to 2

I decided to make my 40th birthday a turning point. I wanted to prove to myself that I can look better and feel better in my 40's. I didn't want to make any more of the excuses that had been stopping me from getting back into shape. The more I saw results, the more my life became more cheerful, colorful, and livelier! And after I finished, I felt fulfilled and complete. Yet I wanted to do it all over again! Now many people see me and compliment my physique and tell me I inspired them. That is the reward I enjoy the most!

Body-*for*-LIFE   The Power Mindset

Please write down 5 things you can do between now and this time tomorrow that will help you move forward in the direction of your 12-week goals.

	PLAN	ACTUAL
1		
2		
3		
4		
5		

Body-*for*-LIFE   The Universal Law of Reciprocation

Please write down 2 things you can do between now and this time tomorrow to support and encourage others.

	PLAN	ACTUAL
1		
2		

Body-*for*-LIFE   Focus on Progress, Not Perfection

Please write down 3 things you did very well today that helped you move toward the achievement of your 12-week goals.

1	
2	
3	

Please write down one thing you will do even better tomorrow.

1	

Notes:

DAY 41

Body-*for*-LIFE   The Eating-*for*-LIFE Method™

PLAN		ACTUAL	
Meal 1		**Meal 1**	
☑ a.m. ☐ p.m.	menTech	☐ a.m. ☐ p.m.	
Meal 2		**Meal 2**	
☐ a.m. ☐ p.m.	myoplex	☐ a.m. ☐ p.m.	
Meal 3		**Meal 3**	
☐ a.m. ☐ p.m.	tri oplex	☐ a.m. ☐ p.m.	
Meal 4		**Meal 4**	
☐ a.m. ☐ p.m.	Trioplex	☐ a.m. ☐ p.m.	
Meal 5		**Meal 5**	
☐ a.m. ☐ p.m.	Grilled chin	☐ a.m. ☐ p.m.	
Meal 6		**Meal 6**	
☐ a.m. ☐ p.m.	mesoTech	☐ a.m. ☐ p.m.	

Notes: thermogen x -2 capsun

Body-*for*-LIFE

The 20-Minute Aerobics Solution™

Intensity Pattern

	PLAN		ACTUAL	
Planned Start Time: 7:00			**Actual Start Time:** 8:05	
Planned End Time: 7:20			**Actual End Time:** 8:25	
Time to Complete: 20 Minutes			**Time to Complete:** 20	

Exercise	Minute by Minute	Intensity Level	Minute by Minute	Intensity Level
	1	5	1	5
	2	5	2	6
	3	6	3	7
	4	7	4	8
	5	8	5	9
P 3 recumbent	6	9	6	5
	7	6	7	6
	8	7	8	7
	9	8	9	8
	10	9	10	9
	11	6	11	5
	12	7	12	6
	13	8	13	
	14	9	14	7
	15	6	15	8
	16	7	16	
	17	8	17	8
High Point	18	9	18	9
	19	10	19	
	20	5	20	5

Notes: 165.5 Nip-cm

5.83 km

320 cal

Bill Phillips — Lesson-*for*-LIFE

"Congratulations! You've now passed the halfway mark!"

Congratulations! You've now passed the halfway mark! You are actually doing it—you're well on your way to achieving your goals! Give yourself a pat on the back! Seriously, I am proud of you. And I'm sure the people around you are proud of you as well. I know you can feel the momentum and positive energy building. Aspects of this Program that were intimidating, confusing, and awkward just six weeks ago are now becoming second nature. You're becoming an expert at taking care of your body, and I know you're already enjoying a higher quality of life. And, as you can clearly see, your body is transforming... you are losing fat, building strength, and gaining energy. So, once again, congratulations! You are on your way, but don't stop now! I encourage you to build on the momentum you've already created and make the next six weeks your best ever!

Success Story — Rodney Latham

Age 32•Lufkin, TX•Respiratory Therapist
Reduced Bodyfat from 20% to 9%
Lost 28 lbs of Fat, Gained 10 lbs of Muscle

Believing that if I finished the Challenge I would look and feel better than ever kept me on track. It was tough at times, but looking back, the 12 weeks went by fast! I now have the self-confidence I need to achieve any goal I set. I have improved my ability to encourage people to reach higher, while learning that an investment made in helping others gives back priceless returns. By far the greatest reward has been the joy and satisfaction I feel when others are inspired to improve themselves after seeing my success story.

Body-*for*-LIFE   The Power Mindset

Please write down 5 things you can do between now and this time tomorrow that will help you move forward in the direction of your 12-week goals.

	PLAN	ACTUAL
1		
2		
3		
4		
5		

Body-*for*-LIFE   The Universal Law of Reciprocation

Please write down 2 things you can do between now and this time tomorrow to support and encourage others.

	PLAN	ACTUAL
1		
2		

Body-*for*-LIFE   Focus on Progress, Not Perfection

Please write down 3 things you did very well today that helped you move toward the achievement of your 12-week goals.

1	
2	
3	

Please write down one thing you will do even better tomorrow.

1	

Notes:

Body-*for*-LIFE The Eating-*for*-LIFE Method™

PLAN	ACTUAL

Meal 1 | **Meal 1**

☐ a.m.
☐ p.m. menocch
+ apple

☐ a.m.
☐ p.m.

Meal 2 | **Meal 2**

☐ a.m. myoplex
☐ p.m.

☐ a.m.
☐ p.m.

Meal 3 | **Meal 3**

☐ a.m. tuna
☐ p.m.

☐ a.m.
☐ p.m.

Meal 4 | **Meal 4**

☐ a.m. Trnplx($\frac{1}{2}$)
☐ p.m.

☐ a.m.
☐ p.m.

Meal 5 | **Meal 5**

☐ a.m. chilin
☐ p.m. veg

☐ a.m.
☐ p.m.

Meal 6 | **Meal 6**

☐ a.m. menocch
☐ p.m.

☐ a.m.
☐ p.m.

Notes: (1)- thermo Rx - 6:00   thermRx 6:45
        f   6:15   CitAAG 7:j.

Body-*for*-LIFE — Upper Body Workout

Intensity Pattern

	PLAN	ACTUAL
Planned Start Time: **6:30**		Actual Start Time: **7:41**
Planned End Time: **7:16**		Actual End Time: **8:35**
Time to Complete: 46 Minutes		Time to Complete: **46'**

Upper Body Muscle Groups	Exercise	Reps	Weight (lbs)	Minutes Between Sets	Intensity Level	Reps	Weight (lbs)	Minutes Between Sets	Intensity Level
Chest	incln	12	40	1	5	12	40	1	5
	bc	10	45	1	6	10	45	1	6
		8	45	1	7 2.0	8	45	1	7
		6	45	1	8 3.40	6	45	1	8
High Point		12	45	0	9 5.00	12	12	8	9
		12	35	2	10	12	8	2	8
Shoulders	military	12	25	1	5 8.41	12	25	1	5
	pm	10	30	1	6 10	10	30	1	6
		8	35	1	7 11.30	8	35	1	7
		6	40	1	8 12.01	6	40	1	8
High Point		12	35	0	9 14-12	12	35	0	5
	dumbell ran	12	10	2	10	12	10	2	8
Back	dumbell	12	40	1	5 18.2	12	40	1	5
	rows	10	45	1	6	10	45	1	6
		8	45	1	7	8	45	1	7
		6	45	1	8 22.20	6	45	1	8
High Point		12	45	0	9	12	45	0	9
	shrugs	12	30	2	10 23.40	12	30	2	8
Triceps	ext	12	25	1	5 27.0	12	21	1	5
		10	25	1	6	10		1	6
		8	25	1	7	8		1	7
		6	25	1	8	6		1	8
High Point		12	20	0	9	12		0	8
	dip	12	12	2	10	12	3-2-1	2	8

At this point, you should be 37 minutes into your upper body workout and have 9 minutes to go.

Biceps	curl	12	20	1	5 32.4	12	20	1	5
		10	25	1	6 38.3	10	25	1	
		8	30	1	7 40.?	8	37	1	
		6	35	1	8 41.0	8	31	1	
High Point		12	30	0	9 43.51	12	30	0	
		12	25	–	10	12		2	

Notes:

Bill Phillips   Lesson-*for*-LIFE

"Consistent variety is the spice of life."

The Body-*for*-LIFE nutrition program is very structured and specific—it is designed to give your body a consistent supply of the nutrients it needs, but it also allows for variety. You don't have to eat the exact same foods day after day. There are many ways you can prepare healthy Body-*for*-LIFE authorized meals. In fact, in my new Body-*for*-LIFE Cookbook, I share over 100 of my favorite Body-*for*-LIFE recipes. By using a variety of cooking techniques, ingredients, spices, and sauces, you can enjoy Body-*for*-LIFE meals more than you enjoyed eating the old way. Throughout this Program, as you consistently enjoy the taste and experience of eating a variety of healthy, nutritious meals, you'll notice that your appetite for junk food goes down while your energy level goes up. So please, be sure to incorporate consistent variety into your Program so it doesn't go stale.

Success Story   Mary Queen

Age 28•High Point, NC•Mother
Gained 9 lbs of Muscle, Lost 23 lbs of Fat

Over 16 months after my daughter was born, I still weighed 25 lbs more than before I was pregnant. That was hurting me emotionally more than anything. I started the Program by viewing the 12 weeks as a series of baby steps—each day, each step, taking me closer to my goal. I have accomplished something important and have discovered that changing yourself physically can uplift your spirits in every way. I can now push myself beyond physical pain and emotional blocks to achieve my goals for life.

Body-*for*-LIFE   The Power Mindset

Please write down 5 things you can do between now and this time tomorrow that will help you move forward in the direction of your 12-week goals.

	PLAN	ACTUAL
1		
2		
3		
4		
5		

Body-*for*-LIFE   The Universal Law of Reciprocation

Please write down 2 things you can do between now and this time tomorrow to support and encourage others.

	PLAN	ACTUAL
1		
2		

Body-*for*-LIFE   Focus on Progress, Not Perfection

Please write down 3 things you did very well today that helped you move toward the achievement of your 12-week goals.

1	
2	
3	

Please write down one thing you will do even better tomorrow.

1	

Notes:

Body-*for*-LIFE   The Eating-*for*-LIFE Method™

PLAN	ACTUAL

Meal 1

☐ a.m.
☐ p.m.   ① meroract

Meal 1

☑ a.m.
☐ p.m.   Pineple
(fish)

Meal 2

☐ a.m.
☐ p.m.   ½ yoprt

Meal 2

☐ a.m.
☐ p.m.   apple

Meal 3

☐ a.m.
☐ p.m.   tbsp ½ Tuna

Meal 3

☐ a.m.
☑ p.m.   tuna

1

Meal 4

☐ a.m.
☐ p.m.   ½ Tuna

Meal 4

☐ a.m.
☑ p.m.   tuna

4

Meal 5

☐ a.m.
☐ p.m.   myopla

Meal 5

☐ a.m.
☑ p.m.   myoph

7:00

Meal 6

☐ a.m.
☐ p.m.   fish/ky

Meal 6

☑ a.m.
☐ p.m.   stew
+
veg 7pm

10

Notes:

Body-*for*-LIFE

The 20-Minute Aerobics Solution™

Intensity Pattern

	PLAN		ACTUAL	
	Planned Start Time: 7:00		Actual Start Time: 7:45	
	Planned End Time: 7:2.		Actual End Time: 8:05	
	Time to Complete: 20 Minutes		Time to Complete: 2.	
Exercise	**Minute by Minute**	**Intensity Level**	**Minute by Minute**	**Intensity Level**
(P₃)	1	5	1	5
	2	5	2	6
	3	6	3	7
	4	7	4	8
	5	8	5	
	6	9	6	9
	7	6	7	5
	8	7	8	6
	9	8	9	7
	10	9	10	8
	11	6	11	9
	12	7	12	5
	13	8	13	6
	14	9	14	
	15	6	15	7
	16	7	16	8
	17	8	17	9
High Point	18	9	18	
	19	10	19	$-9\frac{1}{2}$
	20	5	20	5

Notes: ptynw

5.83 — 6.01

320 cn — (336)

180 — 166 19-20

recov 166 — (137) rst x 2

Bill Phillips   Lesson-*for*-LIFE

"Renew your body; rejuvenate your life!"

Here's an interesting fact about how the human body tends to work: Up until about age 25, the body renews itself—it builds up faster than it breaks down. Unfortunately, after age 25, both men and women slowly but surely begin losing muscle strength and gaining bodyfat. Now, that happens *only* if you don't do something to prevent it. The good news is that modern science has clearly shown that we can not only slow this process, but in some cases reverse it. With an integrated approach to health and fitness, like Body-*for*-LIFE, you can increase muscle strength and decrease bodyfat, improving mental strength as well. So please realize that if you're over the age of 25, you have to work at being healthy, renewing your body, and rejuvenating your energy—but it can be done. And I firmly believe it's never too late to make a change for the better!

Success Story   Larry Hearn

Age 57•Ontario, CA•Ironworker
Lost 23 lbs of Fat, Gained Energy

My wife started this success story. She heard about Body-*for*-LIFE and suggested I try it. I didn't really think I was out of shape, though. She asked me to take my shirt off and pose for just one picture. She had it developed and showed it to me. For a moment, I wondered who that man in the photo was... then I realized it was me! I got to work and in 12 weeks transformed myself from a fat old man to a strong new man. My advice: Take a photo and decide if you want to change or stay the same.

Body-*for*-LIFE   The Power Mindset

Please write down 5 things you can do between now and this time tomorrow that will help you move forward in the direction of your 12-week goals.

	PLAN	ACTUAL
1		
2		
3		
4		
5		

Body-*for*-LIFE   The Universal Law of Reciprocation

Please write down 2 things you can do between now and this time tomorrow to support and encourage others.

	PLAN	ACTUAL
1		
2		

Body-*for*-LIFE   Focus on Progress, Not Perfection

Please write down 3 things you did very well today that helped you move toward the achievement of your 12-week goals.

1	
2	
3	

Please write down one thing you will do even better tomorrow.

1	

Notes:

Body-*for*-LIFE   The Eating-*for*-LIFE Method™

PLAN		ACTUAL	

Meal 1

☑ a.m.
☐ p.m.   mesutci

7:45

Meal 1

☐ a.m.   mesutci
☐ p.m.

Meal 2

☐ a.m.
☐ p.m.   trioptex

10:60

Meal 2

☐ a.m.
☐ p.m.

Meal 3

☐ a.m.
☑ p.m.   tryopta

1

Meal 3

☐ a.m.
☐ p.m.

Meal 4

☐ a.m.
☑ p.m.   myopre

4

Meal 4

☐ a.m.
☐ p.m.

Meal 5

☐ a.m.
☐ p.m.

7

Meal 5

☐ a.m.
☐ p.m.

Meal 6

☐ a.m.
☐ p.m.

10

Meal 6

☐ a.m.
☐ p.m.

Notes:

Body-*for*-LIFE — Lower Body Workout

Intensity Pattern

	PLAN		ACTUAL	
Planned Start Time: 6:30			Actual Start Time: 7:33	
Planned End Time: 7:15			Actual End Time: 8:25	
Time to Complete: 42 Minutes			Time to Complete: 40	

Lower Body Muscle Groups	Exercise	Reps	Weight (lbs)	Minutes Between Sets	Intensity Level	Reps	Weight (lbs)	Minutes Between Sets	Intensity Level
Quads	~~	12	120	1	5	12	120	1	5
		10	125	1	6	10	125	1	6
		8	121	1	7 2.45	8	121	1	7
		6	121	1	8 4.17	6	121	1	8
High Point		12	125	0	9 5.52	12	121	0	9
		12	90	2	10	12	30	2	8
Hamstrings	clmp	12	60	1	5	12	60	1	5
		10	65	1	6	10	65	1	6
		8	90	1	7	8	70	1	7
		6	75	1	8	6	75	1	8
High Point	legs	12	70	0	9	12	90	0	8
		12	35	2	10	12	35	2	8
Calves	☆	12	40	1	5	12	40	1	5
		10	45	1	6	10	45	1	6
		8	41	1	7	8	41	1	7
		6	45	1	8	6	45	0	8
High Point	sign	12	45	0	9	12	45	0	8
		12	40	2	10	12	40	2	8

At this point, you should be 31 minutes into your lower body workout and have 11 minutes to go.

Lower Body Muscle Groups	Exercise	Reps	Weight (lbs)	Minutes Between Sets	Intensity Level	Reps	Weight (lbs)	Minutes Between Sets	Intensity Level
Abs	Pull	(12)	∅	1	5	12	12	1	5
	crm	(10)	∅	1	6	10	10	1	6
		(8)	∅	1	7	8	8	1	7
		(6)	∅	1	8	6	1	1	8
High Point		12	∅	0	9	12	∅	0	8
	flex cru	12		–	10	12		2	8

Notes: -curls - d.H~n.y c
(60)
need to buy more weign for quads

Bill Phillips — Lesson-*for*-LIFE

> "Structure, clear-cut do's and don'ts, and principles give you direction and peace of mind."

When you consciously clarified your goals at the beginning of this Program, and as you keep them in sight on a daily basis, you will notice that you continue to break free from clutter and confusion. And you'll develop more and more clarity as your energy remains focused on achieving your objectives. Not only does this allow you to accomplish extraordinary results in terms of transforming your body, but it also gives you a mental boost. The structure, clear-cut do's and don'ts, and principles of the Body-*for*-LIFE Program give you direction and peace of mind. Today, notice that the structured exercise, nutrition, and mindset techniques you've been applying so far are helping you improve your physical condition and putting your mind at ease. Notice how your efforts are helping you see more clearly and that your energy is rising. Keep it up!

Success Story — Eric Binegar

Age 35 • Fargo, ND • RN/Art Student
Reduced Waistline from 36 to 32 Inches
Lowered Blood Pressure from 134/90 to 116/80

Initially I thought I would have to give up a lot to complete the Body-*for*-LIFE Program. But now I realize I've gained so much from the experience. Not only have I changed the way I look, but my heart, my most important muscle, is healthier as well. I am simply more alive. I had to dig deep to complete this Challenge, and what I found is a new me. Things are clearer and crisper, and colors are more vivid, which is very important to me as an artist. This is a road of enrichment I'm going to keep traveling.

Body-*for*-LIFE The Power Mindset

Please write down 5 things you can do between now and this time tomorrow
that will help you move forward in the direction of your 12-week goals.

	PLAN	ACTUAL
1		
2		
3		
4		
5		

Body-*for*-LIFE The Universal Law of Reciprocation

Please write down 2 things you can do between now and
this time tomorrow to support and encourage others.

	PLAN	ACTUAL
1		
2		

Body-*for*-LIFE Focus on Progress, Not Perfection

Please write down 3 things you did very well today that helped
you move toward the achievement of your 12-week goals.

1	
2	
3	

Please write down one thing you will do even better tomorrow.

1	

Notes:

Body-*for*-LIFE   The Eating-*for*-LIFE Method™

PLAN		ACTUAL	
Meal 1		**Meal 1**	
☑ a.m. ☐ p.m. 8:15	me Mr w	☐ a.m. ☐ p.m.	
Meal 2		**Meal 2**	
☐ a.m. ☐ p.m. 11	Tuns	☐ a.m. ☐ p.m.	
Meal 3		**Meal 3**	
☐ a.m. ☐ p.m. 1	tuns	☐ a.m. ☐ p.m.	
Meal 4		**Meal 4**	
☐ a.m. ☐ p.m. 4	nyoples	☐ a.m. ☐ p.m.	
Meal 5		**Meal 5**	
☐ a.m. ☐ p.m. 7	½ Trips	☐ a.m. ☐ p.m.	
Meal 6		**Meal 6**	
☐ a.m. ☐ p.m. 10	Fish/ves	☐ a.m. ☐ p.m.	

Notes:

Body-*for*-LIFE

The 20-Minute Aerobics Solution™

Intensity Pattern	PLAN		ACTUAL	
	Planned Start Time: 6:30		Actual Start Time: 7:15	
	Planned End Time: 6:50		Actual End Time: 8:15	
	Time to Complete: 20 Minutes		Time to Complete: ____	

Exercise	Minute by Minute	Intensity Level	Minute by Minute	Intensity Level
	1	5	1	5
	2	5	2	6
	3	6	3	7
	4	7	4	
	5	8	5	8
ʳ₃	6	9	6	9
	7	6	7	5
rccmp?	8	7	8	6
	9	8	9	6
	10	9	10	7
	11	6	11	8
	12	7	12	9
	13	8	13	5
	14	9	14	6
	15	6	15	7
	16	7	16	8
	17	8	17	
High Point	18	9	18	9
	19	10	19	$9\frac{1}{2}$
	20	5	20	5

Notes: 5.92
345
185 → 165 → 1:37
19 5 20 → ren × 1"

Bill Phillips Lesson-*for*-LIFE

"Your genetics ensure your success."

I'm often asked, "Do I have to have a certain kind of genetics to dramatically transform my body in 12 weeks?" My answer is, "Yes! You *do* have to have a certain kind of genetics—the kind of genetics human beings have!" You see, Body-*for*-LIFE produces predictable results in virtually every healthy adult human being. Recent scientific discoveries in gene mapping show that you and I are 99% identical in terms of our genetic fingerprint. And while certainly that 1% difference is conspicuous (different height, hair color, eye color, etc.), that does *not* mean that each person responds completely differently to intense exercise and proper nutrition. As you can clearly see in the success stories throughout this book, that 1% difference makes each of our bodies look unique both before and after. However, you can also clearly see evidence of our "99% similarity" in the way we each transformed ourselves as a result of Body-*for*-LIFE.

Success Story Julie Ann Sproles

Age 25•Boise, ID•Student/Office Assistant
Lost 44 lbs While Gaining Energy
Decreased Pant Size from 14/16 to 7/8

After gaining weight during pregnancy, I was looking to make a change. I was unhappy, tired, and cried every time I looked in the mirror. My husband had the book Body-*for*-LIFE, and I began reading it. It showed me a road I could follow, so I started. Some people discouraged me and said I was wasting my time. But I could feel the changes that were occurring. I felt this Program was right—and it was! My weight went from 184 lbs to 140 lbs, I'm in better shape now than before the baby, and I'm happy.

Body-*for*-LIFE The Power Mindset

Please write down 5 things you can do between now and this time tomorrow
that will help you move forward in the direction of your 12-week goals.

	PLAN	ACTUAL
1		
2		
3		
4		
5		

Body-*for*-LIFE The Universal Law of Reciprocation

Please write down 2 things you can do between now and
this time tomorrow to support and encourage others.

	PLAN	ACTUAL
1		
2		

Body-*for*-LIFE Focus on Progress, Not Perfection

Please write down 3 things you did very well today that helped
you move toward the achievement of your 12-week goals.

1	
2	
3	

Please write down one thing you will do even better tomorrow.

1	

Notes:

Body-*for*-LIFE   The Eating-*for*-LIFE Method™

PLAN		ACTUAL	
Meal 1		**Meal 1**	
☐ a.m. ☐ p.m.	*mentll*	☐ a.m. ☐ p.m.	
Meal 2		**Meal 2**	
☐ a.m. ☐ p.m.	*myuphy*	☐ a.m. ☐ p.m.	*½ Triyl*
Meal 3		**Meal 3**	
☐ a.m. ☐ p.m.	*fdn slv*	☐ a.m. ☑ p.m.	*½ Triyl*
Meal 4		**Meal 4**	
☐ a.m. ☐ p.m.	*½ Triplx*	☐ a.m. ☑ p.m.	*zhus oils*
Meal 5		**Meal 5**	
☐ a.m. ☐ p.m.	*cnlr*	☐ a.m. ☑ p.m.	*myupt*
Meal 6		**Meal 6**	
☐ a.m. ☐ p.m.		☑ a.m. ☑ p.m.	*8:00 enrln vs cnyn*

Notes:

Body-*for*-LIFE — Upper Body Workout

Intensity Pattern

PLAN		ACTUAL	
Planned Start Time: _c:60_		Actual Start Time: _6:35_	
Planned End Time: _645_		Actual End Time: _7:__	
Time to Complete: **46 Minutes**		Time to Complete: (_4337_)	

Upper Body Muscle Groups	Exercise	Reps	Weight (lbs)	Minutes Between Sets	Intensity Level	Reps	Weight (lbs)	Minutes Between Sets	Intensity Level
Chest	incline Dr	12	410	1	5	12	40	1	5
		10	45	1	6	10	40	1	6
		8	45	1	7 2.29	8	45	1	9
		6	45	1	8 4.90	6	45	1	8
High Point	flys	12	45	0	9 5.20	12	45	8	8
		12	35	2	10	12	35	2	
Shoulders	military prs	12	20	1	5 3	12	20	1	5
		10	25	1	6 10.20	10	25	1	6
		8	30	1	7 11.2-P	8	30	1	7
		6	35	1	8 12.5	6	35	1	8
High Point	lat rse	12	30	0	9 17.15	12	30	0	8
		12	10	2	10	12	10	2	9
Back	rows	12	40	1	5 17.3	12	40	1	5
		10	45	1	6 10.5	10	45	1	6
		8	45	1	7 20.0	8	41	1	7
		6	45	1	8 21.27	6	41	1	8
High Point	shrug	12	45	0	9 22.45	12	45	0	8
		12	30	2	10	12	12	2	8
Triceps	ext	12	25	1	5	12	25	1	5
		10	25	1	6	18		1	6
		8	25	1	7	9		1	7
		6	25	1	8	6		1	8
High Point	dip	12	25	0	9	12			8
		12	12	2	10	12	12		3

At this point, you should be 37 minutes into your upper body workout and have 9 minutes to go.

Biceps	curls	12	20	1	5	12	20	1	5
		10	25	1	6	10	25	1	6
		8	30	1	7 3x10	8	30	1	9
		6	35	1	8	6	35	1	8
High Point	hmrs	12	30	0	9	12	30	6	1
		12	35	–	10	12	30	2	1

Notes:

Bill Phillips — Lesson-*for*-LIFE

"The healthier and stronger your muscles,
the healthier and stronger your body!"

By now, I am sure you've experienced a significant increase in strength. In fact, right now, if you turn back to Day 1 and look at the weights you were lifting during your first upper body workout and then look at what weights you used in yesterday's workout, you'll see significant progress. That's one of the payoffs of the journal you've been writing—you can *clearly* measure the positive results you're experiencing up to this point. And you can plan upcoming workouts to ensure your strength continues to climb. Remember, wherever you can measure progress, you can make progress. As your muscles are getting stronger, realize you're improving your health in many ways. Your metabolism is increasing, which means you're burning fat faster each and every day and night. The healthier and stronger your muscles, the healthier and stronger your body!

Success Story — Greg Smith

Age 25•Murray, UT•Student
Gained Muscle, Decreased Bodyfat from 15% to 10%

With every new sign of progress, my hunger for more progress grew. During the 12 weeks, I kept reminding myself of what I wanted. I set out to prove to myself that finishing this Program could be done and that I could do it. I had what it took and even surprised myself with the outcome. I feel and know that no matter what happens, I can make it. Other achievements are no longer in the distance; rather, I am now actively pursuing them with the full confidence I need to attain them. I am stronger and better for having had this experience.

Body-*for*-LIFE The Power Mindset

Please write down 5 things you can do between now and this time tomorrow
that will help you move forward in the direction of your 12-week goals.

	PLAN	ACTUAL
1		
2		
3		
4		
5		

Body-*for*-LIFE The Universal Law of Reciprocation

Please write down 2 things you can do between now and
this time tomorrow to support and encourage others.

	PLAN	ACTUAL
1		
2		

Body-*for*-LIFE Focus on Progress, Not Perfection

Please write down 3 things you did very well today that helped
you move toward the achievement of your 12-week goals.

1	
2	
3	

Please write down one thing you will do even better tomorrow.

1	

Notes:

Body-*for*-LIFE The Eating-*for*-LIFE Method™

PLAN	ACTUAL

Meal 1		**Meal 1**	
☐ a.m. ☐ p.m.		☐ a.m. ☐ p.m.	

Meal 2		**Meal 2**	
☐ a.m. ☐ p.m.		☐ a.m. ☐ p.m.	

Meal 3		**Meal 3**	
☐ a.m. ☐ p.m.		☐ a.m. ☐ p.m.	

Meal 4		**Meal 4**	
☐ a.m. ☐ p.m.		☐ a.m. ☐ p.m.	

Meal 5		**Meal 5**	
☐ a.m. ☐ p.m.		☐ a.m. ☐ p.m.	

Meal 6		**Meal 6**	
☐ a.m. ☐ p.m.		☐ a.m. ☐ p.m.	

Notes:

DAY 48

Body-*for*-LIFE | The 20-Minute Aerobics Solution™

Intensity Pattern

	PLAN		ACTUAL	
	Planned Start Time: _____		Actual Start Time: _____	
	Planned End Time: _____		Actual End Time: _____	
	Time to Complete: 20 Minutes		Time to Complete: _____	
Exercise	Minute by Minute	Intensity Level	Minute by Minute	Intensity Level
	1	5	1	5
	2	5	2	6
	3	6	3	7
	4	7	4	8
	5	8	5	9
β 3	6	9	6	5
	7	6	7	6
recumbent	8	7	8	
	9	8	9	7
	10	9	10	8
	11	6	11	9
	12	7	12	
	13	8	13	5
	14	9	14	6
	15	6	15	7
	16	7	16	8
	17	8	17	9
High Point	18	9	18	
	19	10	19	9½
	20	5	20	5

Notes:

_____

_____

_____

_____

_____

_____

Bill Phillips® Lesson-*for*-LIFE

"There's no limit on how much you can change!"

How far do you have to go to create your best body and enjoy an even higher quality of life? Chances are, it's not nearly as far as this success story, Pam Brown. Her transformation says more than I could possibly describe about what's possible when you truly *decide* to change your life and then *act* on that decision, day in and day out!

Success Story   Pam Brown

Age 34•Colorado Springs, CO•BFL Success Coach•Totally Transformed!

My battle with obesity reached a critical point two years ago. I weighed 244 lbs at 49% bodyfat. After my husband, Jim, was diagnosed with a brain tumor, I used food to cope with stress. I ate to stuff the emotions back down. I became depressed, suffered from high blood pressure, chronic migraines, and almost gave up. In early 2000, I came across Body-*for*-LIFE. The before and after success stories sparked a bit of hope that I hadn't felt in a while. I decided to commit to 12 weeks. I didn't approach the Program one day at a time, I approached it *one minute at a time*. By the end of 12 weeks, I had lost 35 lbs. I started a second 12-week Program and reduced my bodyfat to 25%. By the end of my third 12-week Program, I'd lost a total of 96 lbs of bodyfat and gained 16 lbs of muscle. And today I'm in even better shape! I'm helping my husband and others succeed as well. My new purpose in life is to help others and to give them hope!

Body-*for*-LIFE   The Power Mindset

Please write down 5 things you can do between now and this time tomorrow
that will help you move forward in the direction of your 12-week goals.

	PLAN	ACTUAL
1		
2		
3		
4		
5		

Body-*for*-LIFE   The Universal Law of Reciprocation

Please write down 2 things you can do between now and
this time tomorrow to support and encourage others.

	PLAN	ACTUAL
1		
2		

Body-*for*-LIFE   Focus on Progress, Not Perfection

Please write down 3 things you did very well today that helped
you move toward the achievement of your 12-week goals.

1	
2	
3	

Please write down one thing you will do even better tomorrow.

1	

Notes:

Body-*for*-LIFE   The Eating-*for*-LIFE Method™

PLAN	ACTUAL

Meal 1

☐ a.m.
☐ p.m.   mesotech
              T uptr

Meal 1

☐ a.m.   ½ 1rmph
☐ p.m.

              trioplex

Meal 2

☐ a.m.
☐ p.m.   myoplex

Meal 2

☐ a.m.   ½ 1r'ph
☐ p.m.

Meal 3

☐ a.m.   ½ Ten
☐ p.m.

Meal 3   ½ tuna

☐ a.m.
☐ p.m.

Meal 4

☐ a.m.   ½ tun
☐ p.m.

Meal 4

☐ a.m.   ½ Tuna
☐ p.m.

Meal 5

☐ a.m.   A. chicm/tn
☐ p.m.   se.i

Meal 5

☐ a.m.
☐ p.m.

Meal 6

☐ a.m.
☐ p.m.   myoplex

Meal 6   salmn
              + vegetubl
☐ a.m.   + berr2
☐ p.m.

Notes:

Body-*for*-LIFE — Lower Body Workout

Intensity Pattern

	PLAN	ACTUAL
	Planned Start Time: 7:15	Actual Start Time: 8:55
	Planned End Time: 8:03	Actual End Time: 8:31
	Time to Complete: 42 Minutes	Time to Complete: _____

Lower Body Muscle Groups	Exercise	Reps	Weight (lbs)	Minutes Between Sets	Intensity Level	Reps	Weight (lbs)	Minutes Between Sets	Intensity Level
Quads	2 x 7	12	120	1	5	12	120	1	5
		10	125	1	6	10	125	1	6
		8	125	1	7 2:41	8	125	1	7
		6	125	1	8 4.0	6	125	1	8
High Point	squat!	12	125	0	9 5.5	12	125	0	9
	curl!	12	90	2	10	12	125	2	
Hamstrings		12	60	1	5	12	60	1	5
		10	65	1	6	10	65	1	6
		8	90	1	7	8 1:33	90	1	7
		6	75	1	8	6 15.4	75	1	8
High Point	lunge.	12	90	0	9	12 16:35	90 6:73-73	0	9
		12	35	2	10	12	35	2	9
Calves	extensn	12	40	1	5	12	40	1	5
		10	45	1	6 23.6	10	45	1	6
		8	45	1	7 25.4	8	45	1	7
		6	45	1	8 26.	6	45	1	8
High Point	leg curls	12	45	0	9	12	75	0	8
		12	40	2	10	12	35	2	9

At this point, you should be 31 minutes into your lower body workout and have 11 minutes to go.

Lower Body Muscle Groups	Exercise	Reps	Weight (lbs)	Minutes Between Sets	Intensity Level	Reps	Weight (lbs)	Minutes Between Sets	Intensity Level
Abs	reverse	12	0	1	5	12	0	1	5
		10	0	1	6	10		1	6
		8	0	1	7	1		1	7
		6	0	1	8	6		1	8
High Point	pull	12	0	0	9	12		0	9
		12	0	-	10	12			9

Notes:

Bill Phillips — Lesson-*for*-LIFE

"Please don't lose sight of how great your life truly is!"

Maintaining an accurate perspective on your life can be a challenge. Oftentimes we convince ourselves that our lives are so hard, our circumstances so dire, that things couldn't possibly get worse. In times like these, it's vitally important to open your eyes and see the bigger picture. If you look, you will find people who are suffering *true* hardship and are facing adversity so much more challenging than yours. You will find people who would trade places with you in an instant, because, in reality, *you are blessed*, fortunate, and have much to be thankful for! Please don't take your good fortune for granted. Please don't fall into the trap of believing that you are a victim of life. Please don't lose sight on how great your life truly is! And please realize that it is because of adversity that we grow, not in spite of it. Don't let your challenges hold you back; instead, let them fuel your desire to *make the most of your life!*

Success Story — Jim Brown

Age 34•Colorado Springs, CO•Father
Increased Weight from 113 lbs to 170 lbs
Gained over 50 lbs of Muscle!

My life changed completely when I was diagnosed with a brain tumor. Doctors said if I didn't have surgery, I would die. The surgery was followed by complications: I went into a coma for two months. The left side of my body was paralyzed. I couldn't walk or talk. I lost virtually all my muscle. If it wasn't for the support of my wife, Pam, I would have died. It took years, but I built myself back up. Pam became my Success Coach, helping me complete the Body-*for*-LIFE Program. I feel fortunate to be alive *and* living!

Body-*for*-LIFE   The Power Mindset

Please write down 5 things you can do between now and this time tomorrow that will help you move forward in the direction of your 12-week goals.

	PLAN	ACTUAL
1		
2		
3		
4		
5		

Body-*for*-LIFE   The Universal Law of Reciprocation

Please write down 2 things you can do between now and this time tomorrow to support and encourage others.

	PLAN	ACTUAL
1		
2		

Body-*for*-LIFE   Focus on Progress, Not Perfection

Please write down 3 things you did very well today that helped you move toward the achievement of your 12-week goals.

1	
2	
3	

Please write down one thing you will do even better tomorrow.

1	

Notes:

Body-*for*-LIFE — The Eating-*for*-LIFE Method™

PLAN		ACTUAL	
Meal 1		**Meal 1**	
☐ a.m. ☐ p.m.	mesoTech	☐ a.m. ☐ p.m.	myoplx
Meal 2		**Meal 2**	
☐ a.m. ☐ p.m.	½ trioplx	☐ a.m. ☐ p.m.	triuplx
Meal 3		**Meal 3**	
☐ a.m. ☐ p.m.	½ tuna	☐ a.m. ☐ p.m.	turkcl
Meal 4		**Meal 4**	
☐ a.m. ☐ p.m.	½ tuna	☐ a.m. ☐ p.m.	turkey
Meal 5		**Meal 5**	
☐ a.m. ☐ p.m.	myoplx	☐ a.m. ☐ p.m.	fish + vrsctn
Meal 6		**Meal 6**	
☐ a.m. ☐ p.m.	chicken/rolln	☐ a.m. ☐ p.m.	

Notes:

6.05

335

Body-*for*-LIFE

The 20-Minute Aerobics Solution™

Intensity Pattern		

	PLAN	ACTUAL
	Planned Start Time: 6:20	Actual Start Time: 7:50
	Planned End Time: 6:40	Actual End Time: 8:10
	Time to Complete: 20 Minutes	Time to Complete: 20

Exercise	Minute by Minute	Intensity Level	Minute by Minute	Intensity Level
(P3)	1	5	1	5
	2	5	2	6
	3	6	3	7
	4	7	4	8
	5	8	5	
	6	9	6	9
	7	6	7	6
	8	7	8	7
	9	8	9	
	10	9	10	8
	11	6	11	9
	12	7	12	5
	13	8	13	6
	14	9	14	
	15	6	15	7
	16	7	16	8
	17	8	17	9
High Point	18	9	18	
	19	10	19	(10) 187
	20	5	20	5

Notes:

- 6.06 distan
3.35 calou
187 → 174 → 136
15 - 20

Bill Phillips Lesson-*for*-LIFE

"Life works in mysterious ways, but life works."

Okay… here we are… you and I, sharing this experience called Body-*for*-LIFE. How you got to this point in your life, how I got to this point in my life, and how our paths have crossed is somewhat of a mystery. But I have faith there's a reason for everything, and to me that means there's a reason why I've written these words, and a reason why you are reading these words right now. There's also a reason why life has given us the opportunity to learn the lessons we need to learn, the way we need to learn them. I believe it's much more a matter of choice than chance. And so is the future. Whatever your circumstances in life, whatever the condition of your body, consider that you have a *choice* to learn from your past and to have a wonderful, healthy, meaningful future. And remember that although life works in mysterious ways, *life works*.

Success Story Kimberly Ann Davis

Age 39•Alpharetta, GA•Artist
Decreased Bodyfat from 23% to 15%
Gained Strength, Lost 12 lbs of Fat

I had lost all faith in myself, and my lack of self-worth kept causing me to make unwanted choices about my direction in life. I felt I had reached my low point; my nerves were so bad they were affecting my mental and physical health. One day I read "As I See It" by Bill Phillips. I felt a surge of positive energy guiding me in the right direction. I accepted the Challenge and joined a gym, where I received much support. My husband, Scott, also inspired me with his love and support. Now I feel like I am living again!

Body-*for*-LIFE | The Power Mindset

Please write down 5 things you can do between now and this time tomorrow
that will help you move forward in the direction of your 12-week goals.

	PLAN	ACTUAL
1		
2		
3		
4		
5		

Body-*for*-LIFE | The Universal Law of Reciprocation

Please write down 2 things you can do between now and
this time tomorrow to support and encourage others.

	PLAN	ACTUAL
1		
2		

Body-*for*-LIFE | Focus on Progress, Not Perfection

Please write down 3 things you did very well today that helped
you move toward the achievement of your 12-week goals.

1	
2	
3	

Please write down one thing you will do even better tomorrow.

1	

Notes:

Body-*for*-LIFE The Eating-*for*-LIFE Method™

PLAN		ACTUAL	
Meal 1		**Meal 1**	
☑ a.m. ☐ p.m. 7:30	*meotech + [illegible]*	☐ a.m. ☐ p.m.	*[illegible]*
Meal 2		**Meal 2**	
☑ a.m. ☐ p.m.	*[illegible] ½*	☐ a.m. ☐ p.m.	*[illegible]*
Meal 3		**Meal 3**	
☑ a.m. ☐ p.m.	*[illegible] ½*	☐ a.m. ☐ p.m.	*[illegible]*
Meal 4		**Meal 4**	
☐ a.m. ☐ p.m.	*[illegible]*	☐ a.m. ☑ p.m.	*[illegible]*
Meal 5		**Meal 5**	
☐ a.m. ☐ p.m.	*[illegible] [illegible]*	☐ a.m. ☑ p.m.	*[illegible]*
Meal 6		**Meal 6**	
☐ a.m. ☐ p.m.		☐ a.m. ☐ p.m.	*[illegible] [illegible] 2 [illegible]*

Notes:

DAY 52

Body-*for*-LIFE — Upper Body Workout

Intensity Pattern

	PLAN	ACTUAL
Planned Start Time: 6:15		Actual Start Time: 6:15
Planned End Time: 7:01		Actual End Time: 7:01
Time to Complete: 46 Minutes		Time to Complete: 46"

Upper Body Muscle Groups	Exercise	Reps	Weight (lbs)	Minutes Between Sets	Intensity Level	Reps	Weight (lbs)	Minutes Between Sets	Intensity Level
Chest	pross	12	40	1	5	12	40	1	5
		10	45	1	6	10	45	1	6
		8	45	1	7 2.31	8	45	1	7
		6	45	1	8 3.51	6	45	1	3
High Point	FM	12	45	0	9 5.29	12	45	0	9
		12	35	2	10	12	35	2	9
Shoulders	militm pm	12	20	1	5 9.11	12	20	1	5
		10	25	1	6 11.00	10	25	1	6
		8	30	1	7 12.24	8	30	1	4
		6	35	1	8 13.72	6	35	1	8
High Point		12	30	0	9 15.11	12	30	0	9
		12	10	2	10	12	10	2	9
Back	rows	12	40	1	5 18.2	12	40	1	5
		10	45	1	6 20.0	10	45	1	6
		8	45	1	7 21.21	8	41	1	7
		6	45	1	8 25.56	6	40	1	8
High Point	shrug	12	45	0	9 24.09	12	45	0	9
		12	36	2	10	12	30	2	9
Triceps	ext	12	12	1	5 27.11	12	24	1	5
		10	10	1	6	10	12	1	6
		8	8	1	7 31.41	8	11	1	4
		6	6	1	8	6	11	1	8
High Point		12	12	0	9	12	25	0	9
		12	12	2	10	12	15-2	2	9
At this point, you should be 37 minutes into your upper body workout and have 9 minutes to go.									
Biceps	curn	12	20	1	5 38.11	12	20	1	5
		10	25	1	6 35.34	10	21	1	6
		8	30	1	7 21.01	8	30	1	7
		6	35	1	8 42.33	6	35	1	3
High Point	hmm	12	30	0	9	12	30 25.20	0	9
		12	25	–	10	12	15	0	9

Notes: 7 milim pm T 25r

Bill Phillips — Lesson-*for*-LIFE

"Don't 'just do it,' do it with passion and pride!"

So you want to change the way you look? You want to change the way you feel? You want to improve your health? You want to lose fat and gain muscle strength? Good! That's a start. But I need to remind you that actions speak louder than words. You have to talk the talk *and* walk the walk. And you can't just go through the motions. You really do have to put your heart and soul into this. You're going to get out of this what you put into it. So don't "just do it," *do it with passion and pride!* When you truly give it your all, you'll know it; you'll *feel* it inside and *see* it on the outside. And please, don't put yourself in the position where you're looking back at the end of this 12-week Program and wishing you would have tried harder. Today, and every day, give it all you've got… *and more!*

Success Story — Anthony Ellis

Age 26•New York, NY•CPU Graphics Operator
Gained 30 lbs of Muscle While Losing Fat

My transformation proved to me that knowledge isn't power—knowledge applied with passion, desire, and a sense of urgency is power! With my real-life experience, I am helping to inspire many others. When they see an average person like me getting great results, they become believers in the approach *and* believers in themselves. Doing this has been very empowering. I now look at other seemingly unattainable goals as being within my reach. This has lifted my performance in all aspects of my life.

Body-*for*-LIFE The Power Mindset

Please write down 5 things you can do between now and this time tomorrow that will help you move forward in the direction of your 12-week goals.

	PLAN	ACTUAL
1		
2		
3		
4		
5		

Body-*for*-LIFE The Universal Law of Reciprocation

Please write down 2 things you can do between now and this time tomorrow to support and encourage others.

	PLAN	ACTUAL
1		
2		

Body-*for*-LIFE Focus on Progress, Not Perfection

Please write down 3 things you did very well today that helped you move toward the achievement of your 12-week goals.

1	
2	
3	

Please write down one thing you will do even better tomorrow.

1	

Notes:

Body-*for*-LIFE The Eating-*for*-LIFE Method™

PLAN			ACTUAL		
Meal 1			**Meal 1**		
9:0.	☑ a.m. ☐ p.m.	myoplex		☐ a.m. ☐ p.m.	myoplex
Meal 2			**Meal 2**		
11:30	☐ a.m. ☐ p.m.	tuna ~~myoplex~~		☐ a.m. ☐ p.m.	tuna
Meal 3			**Meal 3**		
2:30	☐ a.m. ☐ p.m.	tuna		☐ a.m. ☐ p.m.	tuna
Meal 4			**Meal 4**		
5:0.	☐ a.m. ☐ p.m.	myoplex		☐ a.m. ☐ p.m.	myoplex
Meal 5			**Meal 5**		
7:30	☐ a.m. ☐ p.m.	½ trioplex		☐ a.m. ☐ p.m.	mel~
Meal 6			**Meal 6**		
11:0.	☐ a.m. ☐ p.m.	fish + vegetable		☐ a.m. ☐ p.m.	3 meal pill tuna of past

Notes:

DAY 53

Body-*for*-LIFE

The 20-Minute Aerobics Solution™

Intensity Pattern

PLAN		ACTUAL	
Planned Start Time: 6:30		Actual Start Time: 6:55	
Planned End Time: _____		Actual End Time: 7:15	
Time to Complete: 20 Minutes		Time to Complete: 20	

Exercise	Minute by Minute	Intensity Level	Minute by Minute	Intensity Level
(P3)	1	5	1	5
	2	5	2	6
	3	6	3	7
	4	7	4	8
	5	8	5	9
	6	9	6	
	7	6	7	5
	8	7	8	6
	9	8	9	7
	10	9	10	8
	11	6	11	9
	12	7	12	5
	13	8	13	6
	14	9	14	7
	15	6	15	8
	16	7	16	8
	17	8	17	9
High Point	18	9	18	9
	19	10	19	
	20	5	20	5

Notes: (P3)

5

Bill Phillips — Lesson-*for*-LIFE

> "A strong, energetic body is the best foundation upon which to build success."

Many people, before their Body-*for*-LIFE experience, had been living an unbalanced life, neglecting their health in order to "succeed" in other areas. There's a price to pay for that kind of "success" though, including fatigue, frustration, and even failure. Success in America today seems to follow this line of thinking: "First, get the money, then get the stuff, *then* take care of your body." That just doesn't seem right to me. But I'm surprised at how many people do prioritize the pursuit of material possessions and career advancement over personal health. The way I see it, when you prioritize health and fitness—when you take great care of yourself—success in other areas of life is much more attainable *and* rewarding. In fact, I believe that a strong, energetic body is the best foundation upon which to build success in other areas of your life. At least that's what has worked for me!

Success Story — Karen Bell

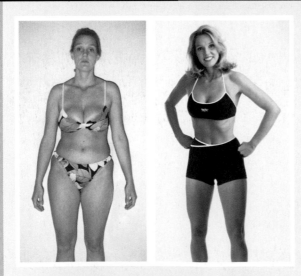

Age 30 • Chandler, AZ • Product Manager/Student
Gained Energy, Lost 14 lbs of Fat

My career left me exhausted and stressed, then a friend showed me the *Body of Work* movie. I couldn't get the idea out of my mind. My desire was solidified the day I saw my before picture. I couldn't believe that was me. I started the Program and soon discovered that exercising cleared my mind. I found myself reconnecting with family and friends I had neglected because of my focus on work. This experience was about more than just wearing a swimsuit again; it was about obtaining balance and success in my life.

Body-*for*-LIFE — The Power Mindset

Please write down 5 things you can do between now and this time tomorrow that will help you move forward in the direction of your 12-week goals.

PLAN	ACTUAL
1	
2	
3	
4	
5	

Body-*for*-LIFE — The Universal Law of Reciprocation

Please write down 2 things you can do between now and this time tomorrow to support and encourage others.

PLAN	ACTUAL
1	
2	

Body-*for*-LIFE — Focus on Progress, Not Perfection

Please write down 3 things you did very well today that helped you move toward the achievement of your 12-week goals.

1
2
3

Please write down one thing you will do even better tomorrow.

1

Notes:

Body-*for*-LIFE | The Eating-*for*-LIFE Method™

PLAN		ACTUAL	
Meal 1		**Meal 1**	
☑ a.m. ☐ p.m.	*mesulcu*	☐ a.m. ☐ p.m.	
Meal 2		**Meal 2**	
☐ a.m. ☐ p.m.	*on ½ yogurte*	☐ a.m. ☐ p.m.	
Meal 3		**Meal 3**	
☐ a.m. ☐ p.m.	*fishn*	☐ a.m. ☐ p.m.	
Meal 4		**Meal 4**	
☐ a.m. ☐ p.m.		☐ a.m. ☐ p.m.	
Meal 5		**Meal 5**	
☐ a.m. ☐ p.m.	*chrcn + ycs*	☐ a.m. ☐ p.m.	
Meal 6		**Meal 6**	
☐ a.m. ☐ p.m.		☐ a.m. ☐ p.m.	

Notes:

Body-*for*-LIFE   Lower Body Workout

Intensity Pattern

	PLAN	ACTUAL
Planned Start Time: _c:15_		Actual Start Time: _c:25_
Planned End Time: _c:49_		Actual End Time: _7:12_
Time to Complete: 42 Minutes		Time to Complete: _____

Lower Body Muscle Groups	Exercise	Reps	Weight (lbs)	Minutes Between Sets	Intensity Level	Reps	Weight (lbs)	Minutes Between Sets	Intensity Level
Quads		12	120	1	5	12	120	1	5
	ex7	10	125	1	6	10	125	1	6
		8	125	1	7	8 2.15	125	1	7
		6	125	1	8	6 4.13	125	1	7
High Point	squats	12	125	0	9	125,56	125	0	9
		12	90	2	10	12	90	2	
Hamstrings	curls	12	60	1	5 9.54	12	60	1	5
		10	65	1	6 11.40	10	65	1	6
		8	70	1	7 13.15	8	70	1	7
		6	75	1	8 14.50	6	75	1	8
High Point	lunges	12	90	0	9	12	70	0	9
		12	35	2	10	12	35	2	9
Calves	ex7	12	40	1	5	12 22.55	40	1	5
		10	45	1	6	10 25.55	45	1	6
		8	45	1	7	8 25.55	45	1	7
		6	45	1	8	6 27.30	45	1	8
High Point	1- ex7	12	45	0	9	12 20.5	45	0	9
		12	45	2	10	12	45	2	9

At this point, you should be 31 minutes into your lower body workout and have 11 minutes to go.

Lower Body Muscle Groups	Exercise	Reps	Weight (lbs)	Minutes Between Sets	Intensity Level	Reps	Weight (lbs)	Minutes Between Sets	Intensity Level
Abs	revers	12	12	1	5	12	0	1	5
		10	10	1	6	10	0	1	6
		8	8	1	7	8	0	1	7
		6	6	1	8	6	0	1	8
High Point	balls	12	12	0	9			0	9
		12	12	–	10			2	9

Notes: _curls -9.1 -12 5s_
_1 ex7 17 (40)_

Bill Phillips — Lesson-*for*-LIFE

"You can only rise as high as your lowest habit."

The person you see in a before photo is a reflection of that person's patterns of action—their habits, the things they do day in and day out without even thinking about them. In order to transform from before to after, those habits need to change. They, like sandbags tied to a hot air balloon, limit your ascent to a higher quality of life. Low-level habits create low-level living. High-level habits allow you to rise up and reach higher and higher. With that in mind, today I ask that you please give consideration to your "lowest level" habit, become even more aware of it, and become more determined to transform that negative habit into a positive pattern of action. As you continue on, you will find that you must constantly transform your habits in order to ascend and reach higher and higher. It's not easy, but I know you can do it!

Success Story — Dr. Bob Karlin

Age 53•Jenkintown, PA•Psychologist
Decreased Bodyfat from 25% to 11%

I feared I was dying and wouldn't even see my daughter finish her first semester of college. A lengthy, draining divorce was concluding; I felt lousy and depressed, was eating poorly, had gotten fat, and had let my health and psychology practice deteriorate. The good news was that I wasn't dead... yet! I decided to do something about it. Now my whole life has turned around. I take good care of myself, and I'm no longer neglectful. I eat healthily, get a full night's sleep, and exercise daily—all new habits.

Body-*for*-LIFE The Power Mindset

Please write down 5 things you can do between now and this time tomorrow
that will help you move forward in the direction of your 12-week goals.

PLAN	ACTUAL
1	
2	
3	
4	
5	

Body-*for*-LIFE The Universal Law of Reciprocation

Please write down 2 things you can do between now and
this time tomorrow to support and encourage others.

PLAN	ACTUAL
1	
2	

Body-*for*-LIFE Focus on Progress, Not Perfection

Please write down 3 things you did very well today that helped
you move toward the achievement of your 12-week goals.

1.
2.
3.

Please write down one thing you will do even better tomorrow.

1.

Notes:

Body-*for*-LIFE   The Eating-*for*-LIFE Method™

PLAN	ACTUAL

Meal 1

☐ a.m.
☐ p.m.

Meal 1

☐ a.m.
☐ p.m.

Meal 2

☐ a.m.
☐ p.m.

Meal 2

☐ a.m.
☐ p.m.

Meal 3

☐ a.m.
☐ p.m.

Meal 3

☐ a.m.
☐ p.m.

Meal 4

☐ a.m.
☐ p.m.

Meal 4

☐ a.m.
☐ p.m.

Meal 5

☐ a.m.
☐ p.m.

Meal 5

☐ a.m.
☐ p.m.

Meal 6

☐ a.m.
☐ p.m.

Meal 6

☐ a.m.
☐ p.m.

Notes:

Body-*for*-LIFE

The 20-Minute Aerobics Solution™

Intensity Pattern

PLAN		ACTUAL	
Planned Start Time: 7:30		Actual Start Time: 8:30	
Planned End Time: 7:50		Actual End Time: 8:50	
Time to Complete: 20 Minutes		Time to Complete: 2.	

Exercise	Minute by Minute	Intensity Level	Minute by Minute	Intensity Level
	1	5	1	5
	2	5	2	
	3	6	3	6
	4	7	4	7
	5	8	5	8
P3	6	9	6	9
recumbent	7	6	7	5
level	8	7	8	6
	9	8	9	
	10	9	10	7
	11	6	11	8
	12	7	12	
	13	8	13	9
	14	9	14	5
	15	6	15	6
	16	7	16	7
	17	8	17	8
High Point	18	9	18	9
	19	10	19	9
	20	5	20	5

Notes: dist 6.02 335 w? 166lp

Bill Phillips — Lesson-*for*-LIFE

"As you move closer and closer to your deadline, you'll notice your intensity picking up."

One of the things I've learned over the years is that setting deadlines is perhaps the most powerful motivator there is. That's why with Body-*for*-LIFE we set a *specific* deadline for when we're going to finish. Knowing exactly when you've decided to take that after photo will allow you to harness the power of positive pressure. In fact, as you move closer and closer to your deadline, you'll notice your intensity picking up. Many of the success stories I've reviewed note that their focus increased so much during their last month of the Program that they were able to make as many positive changes during the final four weeks as during the previous eight! So today, please make sure you're aware of your deadline for finishing this Program. Notice that you've got only four weeks to go! Look forward to your deadline, and allow it to give you a burst of energy as you head down the final stretch!

Success Story — Tom Archipley

**Age 32•Okemos, MI•Pre-Med Student
Gained 9 lbs of Muscle, Lost 30 lbs of Fat**

By setting goals and committing to a specific deadline, I've learned you can find time where there used to be none. You can find inner strength where there used to be excuses. You can find confidence where there used to be self-doubt. You can find your hidden potential and become a stronger, better person. That's the way the Challenge worked for me. This whole experience has helped me confront my fear of failure and has helped me develop character along with my body and health.

Body-*for*-LIFE   The Power Mindset

Please write down 5 things you can do between now and this time tomorrow
that will help you move forward in the direction of your 12-week goals.

	PLAN	ACTUAL
1		
2		
3		
4		
5		

Body-*for*-LIFE   The Universal Law of Reciprocation

Please write down 2 things you can do between now and
this time tomorrow to support and encourage others.

	PLAN	ACTUAL
1		
2		

Body-*for*-LIFE   Focus on Progress, Not Perfection

Please write down 3 things you did very well today that helped
you move toward the achievement of your 12-week goals.

1	
2	
3	

Please write down one thing you will do even better tomorrow.

1	

Notes:

DAY 57

Body-*for*-LIFE | The Eating-*for*-LIFE Method™

PLAN	ACTUAL

Meal 1
- ☑ a.m.
- ☐ p.m.
- 8:00

merotech

Meal 1
- ☐ a.m.
- ☐ p.m.

Me9rx

Meal 2
- ☑ a.m.
- ☐ p.m.
- 15:05

myoplex

Meal 2
- ☐ a.m.
- ☐ p.m.

myoplex

Meal 3
- ☑ a.m.
- ☐ p.m.
- 15:00

Me9rx
graham
cracker

Meal 3
- ☐ a.m.
- ☐ p.m.

sandwich
grilled chm
w.a fr

Meal 4
- ☑ a.m.
- ☐ p.m.
- 8:30

myoplex

Meal 4
- ☐ a.m.
- ☐ p.m.

myoplex

Meal 5
- ☐ a.m.
- ☐ p.m.
- 7:00

chicken
+
salad

Meal 5
- ☐ a.m.
- ☐ p.m.

Meal 6
- ☐ a.m.
- ☐ p.m.

Meal 6
- ☐ a.m.
- ☐ p.m.

meqbls
chkn
rn m
14-cr X

Notes: w1 168 llb

Body-*for*-LIFE — Upper Body Workout

Intensity Pattern

	PLAN	ACTUAL
Planned Start Time: 7:30		Actual Start Time: _____
Planned End Time: 8:16		Actual End Time: _____
Time to Complete: 46 Minutes		Time to Complete: 45 31

Upper Body Muscle Groups	Exercise	Reps	Weight (lbs)	Minutes Between Sets	Intensity Level	Reps	Weight (lbs)	Minutes Between Sets	Intensity Level
Chest	inclin BP	12	40	1	5	12	40	1	5
		10	45	1	6	10	45	1	6
		8	45	1	7 2:20 8		45	1	9
		6	45	1	8 3:18 6		41	1	8
High Point	five	12	45	0	9 5:04 12		41	0	8
		12	⃝40	2	10	12	40	2	8
Shoulders	press mil	12	25	1	5 9:42 12		25	1	5
		10	30	1	6 11:8 10		30	1	6
		8	35	1	7 12:31 8		35	1	7
		6	40	1	8 14:	1	40 2:74	1	8
High Point	1+1 ram	12	35	0	9	12	3⃝0	0	8
		12	10	2	10	12	10	2	9
Back	row	12	40	1	5	12	40	⃝1	5
		10	45	1	6 20:71	10	45	1	6
		8	45	1	7 22:01 8		45	1	7
		6	45	1	8 23:40 6		45	1	8
High Point	shrug.	12	45	0	9 25:44	12	45	⃝1	9
		12	35	2	10	12	35	2	9
Triceps	ext	12	25	1	5 28:19	12	25	⃝1	5
		10	25	1	6 29:46	10		1	6
		8	25	1	7 31:21	8		1	7
		6	25	1	8 32:55	6		1	8
High Point	dip?	12	25	0	9 33:5	12	25	⃝0	
		12	12	2	10	12	12	2	

At this point, you should be 37 minutes into your upper body workout and have 9 minutes to go.

Biceps	curls	12	20	1	5 37:0	12	20	1	5
		10	25	1	6 39:11	10	25	1	6
		8	30	1	7 40:00	8	30	1	7
		6	35	1	8 41:05 43:0	6	32	1	8
High Point	hammer curl	12	30	0	9	12	30	0	0
		12	25	–	10	12	20	0	0

Notes:

Bill Phillips — Lesson-*for*-LIFE

"There's no such thing as an easy challenge."

I'm often asked, "Bill, isn't there an easier way to get in shape than Body-*for*-LIFE?" My answer: "If there is, I don't know about it." Seriously, I really don't know of a way to dramatically transform your body, in as little as 12 weeks, that works better than Body-*for*-LIFE. And I also don't know of an "easy" way to do it. In fact, that's why I call Body-*for*-LIFE "The Challenge." It's not easy. However, living life in a body you don't like—a body that doesn't feel good—*isn't easy either!* I can't tell you there's an easy way out, but there *is* a way out. It's worth the effort. Ask those who've completed the Body-*for*-LIFE Program and become success stories… They will tell you that the Program was less of a challenge than continuing on in the direction they were going before. When you finish, you'll know what we mean.

Success Story — Linda Kelley-Catlow

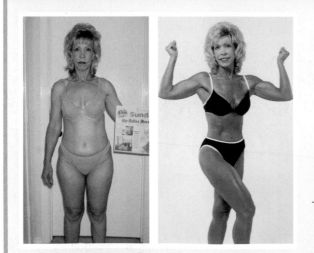

Age 52•McKinney, TX•Admin. Assistant
Lost 20 lbs of Fat, Decreased Bodyfat by 17%
Transformed from an 8/9 to a 4/5 Dress Size

I knew I needed to change something, but the fact that I had tried and failed with numerous "easy diets" in the past left me discouraged. When I looked at the Body-*for*-LIFE approach, I saw real people, of all shapes and sizes, working hard, challenging themselves, and succeeding. I felt I could do it too. I was ready to get to work, so I accepted Bill's Challenge. The person you see in my after photo is the result. And the best reward is that I'm now inspiring others to look and feel better too. That makes me feel proud.

Body-*for*-LIFE   The Power Mindset

Please write down 5 things you can do between now and this time tomorrow
that will help you move forward in the direction of your 12-week goals.

	PLAN	ACTUAL
1		
2		
3		
4		
5		

Body-*for*-LIFE   The Universal Law of Reciprocation

Please write down 2 things you can do between now and
this time tomorrow to support and encourage others.

	PLAN	ACTUAL
1		
2		

Body-*for*-LIFE   Focus on Progress, Not Perfection

Please write down 3 things you did very well today that helped
you move toward the achievement of your 12-week goals.

1	
2	
3	

Please write down one thing you will do even better tomorrow.

1	

Notes:

Body-*for*-LIFE   The Eating-*for*-LIFE Method™

PLAN		ACTUAL	
Meal 1		**Meal 1**	
☐ a.m. ☐ p.m.		☐ a.m. ☐ p.m.	
Meal 2		**Meal 2**	
☐ a.m. ☐ p.m.		☐ a.m. ☐ p.m.	myuplii
Meal 3		**Meal 3**	
☐ a.m. ☐ p.m.		☐ a.m. ☐ p.m.	TurM
Meal 4		**Meal 4**	
☐ a.m. ☐ p.m.		☐ a.m. ☐ p.m.	TurM
Meal 5		**Meal 5**	
☐ a.m. ☐ p.m.		☐ a.m. ☐ p.m.	Mcl~
Meal 6		**Meal 6**	
☐ a.m. ☐ p.m.		☑ a.m. ☑ p.m. 1c.u	meanloll

Notes: _Themp. R_
_1.69.5_

Body-*for*-LIFE | The 20-Minute Aerobics Solution™

Intensity Pattern

	PLAN		ACTUAL	
Planned Start Time: 6:15			**Actual Start Time:** 8:00	
Planned End Time: 6:25			**Actual End Time:** 8:20	
Time to Complete: 20 Minutes			**Time to Complete:** _____	

Exercise	Minute by Minute	Intensity Level	Minute by Minute	Intensity Level
	1	5	1	5
	2	5	2	
	3	6	3	6
P3	4	7	4	7
	5	8	5	
recumb	6	9	6	8
	7	6	7	9
	8	7	8	5
	9	8	9	
	10	9	10	6
	11	6	11	7
	12	7	12	8
	13	8	13	9
	14	9	14	9
	15	6	15	6
	16	7	16	7
	17	8	17	9
High Point	18	9	18	
	19	10	19	8
	20	5	20	5

Notes:

5.89

320 cal

recum 177

not a good
effort

186

Bill Phillips | Lesson-*for*-LIFE

"Keep the momentum going and the energy flowing!"

Let's talk a little basic physics—getting an object at rest to begin moving requires far more energy than it does to keep it moving. Think of a rocket: 90% of the energy is spent on the initial thrust—on getting the blasted thing into the air. The remaining 10% is all that's needed to keep it going. In a way, the same applies to transforming our bodies—it's the act of getting started that is, by far, the most challenging stage of the process. You are experiencing considerable momentum at this point, and you are in a position to make an extraordinary transformation. But, if you were to stop now, you would lose all that momentum and you would have to start all over again. I don't want you to have to go through that, and I know you don't either. So please, *hang in there!* Keep the momentum going and the energy flowing!

Success Story | Gary and Amy Arbuckle

Ages 28 and 24•Denver, CO
Parents/Doctor and Weather Anchor
Combined, Gained 20 lbs of Muscle
Lost 48 lbs of Fat

To do this Program together, we had to juggle our schedules and learn how to plan our meals and workouts. As working parents, it was hard at first to make time. But after a few weeks, we began seeing results in each other, and we knew this was working. We were losing fat and getting stronger. Then the positive energy propelled us forward and helped us finish strong! We are now better parents, more confident in our careers, and are able to help others transform themselves.

Body-*for*-LIFE — The Power Mindset

Please write down 5 things you can do between now and this time tomorrow
that will help you move forward in the direction of your 12-week goals.

	PLAN	ACTUAL
1		
2		
3		
4		
5		

Body-*for*-LIFE — The Universal Law of Reciprocation

Please write down 2 things you can do between now and
this time tomorrow to support and encourage others.

	PLAN	ACTUAL
1		
2		

Body-*for*-LIFE — Focus on Progress, Not Perfection

Please write down 3 things you did very well today that helped
you move toward the achievement of your 12-week goals.

1	
2	
3	

Please write down one thing you will do even better tomorrow.

1	

Notes:

Body-*for*-LIFE   The Eating-*for*-LIFE Method™

PLAN		ACTUAL	
Meal 1		**Meal 1**	
☐ a.m. ☐ p.m.		☐ a.m. ☐ p.m.	
Meal 2		**Meal 2**	
☐ a.m. ☐ p.m.		☐ a.m. ☐ p.m.	
Meal 3		**Meal 3**	
☐ a.m. ☐ p.m.		☐ a.m. ☐ p.m.	
Meal 4		**Meal 4**	
☐ a.m. ☐ p.m.		☐ a.m. ☐ p.m.	
Meal 5		**Meal 5**	
☐ a.m. ☐ p.m.		☐ a.m. ☐ p.m.	
Meal 6		**Meal 6**	
☐ a.m. ☐ p.m.		☐ a.m. ☐ p.m.	

Notes:

Body-*for*-LIFE — Lower Body Workout

Intensity Pattern

	PLAN	ACTUAL
Planned Start Time: 6:15		Actual Start Time: 6:25
Planned End Time: 7:50		Actual End Time: 8:05
Time to Complete: 42 Minutes		Time to Complete: 35

Lower Body Muscle Groups	Exercise	Reps	Weight (lbs)	Minutes Between Sets	Intensity Level	Reps	Weight (lbs)	Minutes Between Sets	Intensity Level
Quads	ex	12	120	1	5	12	120	1	5
		10	125	1	6	10	125	1	5
		8	125	1	7 24	8	125	1	7
		6	125	1	8 4.1	6	125	1	8
High Point	sq-w	12	125	0	9	12	125	0	8
		12	90	2	10	12	90	2	9
Ham-strings	sq-m	12	60	1	5 3.2	12	60	1	5
		10	65	1	6 12.4	10	65	1	6
		8	70	1	7 14.2	8	70	1	4
		6	75	1	8	6	75	1	8
High Point		12	70	0	9 15.5	12	70	0	8
		12	35	2	10	12	35	2	9
Calves	ex	12	40	1	5 2.2	12	40	1	5
		10	45	1	6 22.3	10	45	1	6
		8		1	7	8	41	1	7
		6		1	8 2.5 3	6	41	1	8
High Point	1 w	12		0	9	12	45	0	8
		12	45	2	10	12	40	2	8

At this point, you should be 31 minutes into your lower body workout and have 11 minutes to go.

Abs	DC11	12	x	1	5	12	32.5 0	1	5
		10	6	1	6	10	34.06	1	6
		8		1	7	8	35 40	1	7
		6		1	8	6	35 40	1	
High Point		12		0	9	12	32 0	0	
		12		–	10	12	0	2	

Notes:

Bill Phillips — Lesson-*for*-LIFE

"One of the best ways to learn is to teach."

Now that you're well on your way to completing the 12-week Program, you've learned numerous lessons through your personal experiences that can benefit others. I would now like to ask you to help me teach others how to make it through the 12-week Program. One of the ways you can help is to join me online at www.HighPointMedia.com and simply share a lesson you've learned on our message board, "The Empowering Thoughts Forum." Here people like us gather and share uplifting thoughts, ideas, and information. You might be able to teach other people to create the time for exercise and smart nutrition. Maybe you've learned some things about goal setting that have given you an advantage. Perhaps you've learned some things about keeping a positive mindset. If so, *please* accept this invitation to share your empowering thoughts and knowledge with others.

Success Story — Bill Yeager

Age 23 • Plantsville, CT • Contractor
Reduced Waist Size from 37" to 30"
Gained Muscle, Lost 22 lbs of Fat

My whole life I've felt as though my purpose for being on this earth is to touch other people's lives. Before I did the Body-*for*-LIFE Program, I was still searching. The reactions toward my transformation made me realize my purpose. I'm here to help ordinary people like me become stronger and healthier. I've empowered freinds and family and helped them with their transformations. I feel so confident in myself to set goals and acheive them in all aspects of my life. Everywhere I go, I now hold my head up high and smile.

Body-*for*-LIFE | The Power Mindset

Please write down 5 things you can do between now and this time tomorrow
that will help you move forward in the direction of your 12-week goals.

	PLAN	ACTUAL
1		
2		
3		
4		
5		

Body-*for*-LIFE | The Universal Law of Reciprocation

Please write down 2 things you can do between now and
this time tomorrow to support and encourage others.

	PLAN	ACTUAL
1		
2		

Body-*for*-LIFE | Focus on Progress, Not Perfection

Please write down 3 things you did very well today that helped
you move toward the achievement of your 12-week goals.

1		
2		
3		

Please write down one thing you will do even better tomorrow.

1	

Notes:

Body-*for*-LIFE   The Eating-*for*-LIFE Method™

PLAN	ACTUAL
Meal 1	**Meal 1**
☐ a.m. ☐ p.m.	☐ a.m. ☐ p.m. myoplx
Meal 2	**Meal 2**
☐ a.m. ☐ p.m.	☐ a.m. ☐ p.m. tuns
Meal 3	**Meal 3**
☐ a.m. ☐ p.m.	☐ a.m. ☐ p.m. tuns
Meal 4	**Meal 4**
☐ a.m. ☐ p.m.	☐ a.m. ☐ p.m. myoplex
Meal 5	**Meal 5**
☐ a.m. ☐ p.m.	☐ a.m. ☐ p.m.
Meal 6	**Meal 6**
☐ a.m. ☐ p.m.	☐ a.m. ☐ p.m. chickn

Notes:

Body-for-LIFE

The 20-Minute Aerobics Solution™

	PLAN		ACTUAL	
Intensity Pattern 	Planned Start Time: _____		Actual Start Time: _____	
	Planned End Time: _____		Actual End Time: _____	
	Time to Complete: 20 Minutes		Time to Complete: _____	
Exercise	Minute by Minute	Intensity Level	Minute by Minute	Intensity Level
	1	5	1	5
	2	5	2	6
	3	6	3	7
	4	7	4	8
	5	8	5	9
	6	9	6	
3	7	6	7	5 / 6
	8	7	8	7
	9	8	9	8
	10	9	10	9
	11	6	11	5
	12	7	12	
	13	8	13	6
	14	9	14	7
	15	6	15	
	16	7	16	8
	17	8	17	9
High Point	18	9	18	
	19	10	19	8½
	20	5	20	5

Notes:
_____
_____
_____
_____
_____
_____

Bill Phillips Lesson-*for*-LIFE

"To care for others, you must care for yourself."

People care about you and count on you. Friends, family, and co-workers need you even more than you might realize. And in times of crisis and unexpected adversity, you'll be needed even more. It's important to realize that the extent to which you can care for and help others will be determined by how much you care for yourself. If your energy is low, and you're feeling weak and aren't living up to your potential, you may be inadvertently hurting others as well. Likewise, if you are healthy, strong, and have energy to spare, you will be able to reach down and lift others up. Your physical and mental strength are improving every day as a result of your efforts. Please give yourself credit for making it this far. And please recommit to completing this Program with the understanding that this is one of the *best* things you can do to help not just yourself, but those around you!

Success Story Gail Gosselin

Age 32•Dade City, FL•Marketing Rep.
Gained Energy, Lost 30 lbs of Fat

When my mother became terminally ill with cancer, I began venting the stress by eating uncontrollably. The weight I was gaining left me so weak and exhausted that it became a struggle to make it through each day with any energy at all. It was then that I decided I had to change. How could I take care of Mom if I couldn't even take care of myself? I had more than enough reasons to accept Bill's Challenge. As the weeks went by, I gained back my energy and was able to give my mom the best I had to give.

Body-*for*-LIFE   The Power Mindset

Please write down 5 things you can do between now and this time tomorrow
that will help you move forward in the direction of your 12-week goals.

	PLAN	ACTUAL
1		
2		
3		
4		
5		

Body-*for*-LIFE   The Universal Law of Reciprocation

Please write down 2 things you can do between now and
this time tomorrow to support and encourage others.

	PLAN	ACTUAL
1		
2		

Body-*for*-LIFE   Focus on Progress, Not Perfection

Please write down 3 things you did very well today that helped
you move toward the achievement of your 12-week goals.

1	
2	
3	

Please write down one thing you will do even better tomorrow.

1	

Notes:

DAY 61

Body-for-LIFE — The Eating-for-LIFE Method™

PLAN		ACTUAL	
Meal 1		**Meal 1**	
☑ a.m. ☐ p.m. 7 0,0	mented	☐ a.m. ☐ p.m.	1 Metrx
Meal 2		**Meal 2**	
☐ a.m. ☐ p.m. 10 ins	Metra	☐ a.m. ☐ p.m.	½
Meal 3		**Meal 3**	
☐ a.m. ☑ p.m. 1	Grilled Fish chen ro.1	☐ a.m. ☐ p.m.	
Meal 4		**Meal 4**	
☐ a.m. ☑ p.m. 4	myoph	☐ a.m. ☐ p.m.	grilled chen salad
Meal 5		**Meal 5**	
☐ a.m. ☑ p.m. 7	chen/fish salad	☐ a.m. ☐ p.m.	½ mtrx
Meal 6		**Meal 6**	
☐ a.m. ☐ p.m.	myoph	☐ a.m. ☐ p.m. ✗	chickn small ice crem pnzco + slice

Notes:

Body-*for*-LIFE — Upper Body Workout

Intensity Pattern

PLAN	ACTUAL
Planned Start Time: 6:00	Actual Start Time: 6:20
Planned End Time: 6:4_	Actual End Time: 7:0_
Time to Complete: 46 Minutes	Time to Complete: 45

Upper Body Muscle Groups	Exercise	Reps	Weight (lbs)	Minutes Between Sets	Intensity Level	Reps	Weight (lbs)	Minutes Between Sets	Intensity Level
Chest	— incln	12	40	1	5	12	40	1	5
	BT	10	45	1	6	10	45	1	6
		8	45	1	7 2.2"	9	48	1	7
		6	31	1	8 4	6	45	1	8
High Point	— crun fly	12	45	0	9 Si25	12	45	0	9
		12	45	2	10	12	54	2	
Shoulders	mility	12	26	1	5 9.21	22	25	1	5
	p'n	10	30	1	6	10	30	1	6
		8	35	1	7 12.7S	8	31	1	7
		6	39	1	8 14.1	6	40	1	8
High Point	lat rsn	12	35	0	9 16:	12	31	0	3
		12	10	2	10	12	10	2	5
Back	rws	12	40	1	5 14	12	40	1	5
		10	45	1	6 20:30	10	45	1	6
		8	45	1	22.cn	8	41	1	7
		6	45	1	8	6	45	1	8
High Point	shrugs	12	45	0	9	12	41	0	3
		12	30	2	10	14	30	2	3
Triceps	ext	12	25	1	5 27.8	12	25	1	5
		10	25	1	6	10	25	1	6
		8	25	1	7 29.0	9	25	1	4
		6	25	1	8	6	25	1	4
High Point	dips	12	25	0	9	13	25	0	3
		12	25	2	10	12	0	2	9

At this point, you should be 37 minutes into your upper body workout and have 9 minutes to go.

Biceps	Hamer curl	12	20	1	5 37	12	20	1	5
		10	25	1	6 38.2	10	25	1	
		8	30	1	7 39	9	30	1	7
		6	35	1	8 41.19	6	35	1	35
High Point		12	30	0	9 42	12	35-25-20	6	30-25-20
		12	35	–	10	12	20-15	2	20-15

Notes:

Bill Phillips — Lesson-*for*-LIFE

"Focus your mind on positive, uplifting
thoughts, images, and expectations!"

From time to time, people may discourage or even criticize you. But instead of allowing others to give you a negative attitude, try to create the opposite effect. When you feel at all put down, lift yourself up by doing something positive for someone or saying something positive to someone. Make this a habit, and it will help give you the energy to move ahead!

Success Story — Kimberly Cantergiani

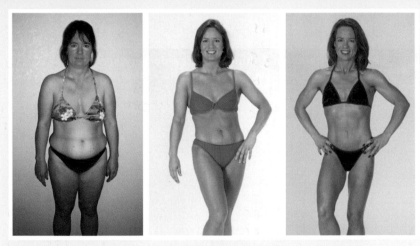

Age 34 • Edinburg, TX • Mother
Decreased Bodyfat from 30% to 10%, Lost 33 lbs of Fat, Gained 7 lbs of Muscle

As a mother of six, it seemed that every month I was losing more control and gaining more weight. And I was developing a negative attitude. The good news is that, as the result of accepting the Challenge to complete two back-to-back, 12-week Body-*for*-LIFE Programs, I not only completely changed my body and look, and feel years younger, but I discovered something very important: that self-mastery and self-control, when achieved in one area of your life, quickly spread to all facets. I now have so much more positive energy to offer those around me whom I care for and who care for me. My energy is boundless, endless. I have a strong sense of purpose and have achieved the balance to create a better life for others and, indirectly, for myself.

Body-*for*-LIFE — The Power Mindset

Please write down 5 things you can do between now and this time tomorrow that will help you move forward in the direction of your 12-week goals.

	PLAN	ACTUAL
1		
2		
3		
4		
5		

Body-*for*-LIFE — The Universal Law of Reciprocation

Please write down 2 things you can do between now and this time tomorrow to support and encourage others.

	PLAN	ACTUAL
1		
2		

Body-*for*-LIFE — Focus on Progress, Not Perfection

Please write down 3 things you did very well today that helped you move toward the achievement of your 12-week goals.

1	
2	
3	

Please write down one thing you will do even better tomorrow.

1	

Notes:

Body-*for*-LIFE   The Eating-*for*-LIFE Method™

PLAN		ACTUAL	
Meal 1		**Meal 1**	
☐ a.m. ☐ p.m.		☐ a.m. ☐ p.m.	
Meal 2		**Meal 2**	
☐ a.m. ☐ p.m.		☐ a.m. ☐ p.m.	
Meal 3		**Meal 3**	
☐ a.m. ☐ p.m.		☐ a.m. ☐ p.m.	
Meal 4		**Meal 4**	
☐ a.m. ☐ p.m.		☐ a.m. ☐ p.m.	
Meal 5		**Meal 5**	
☐ a.m. ☐ p.m.		☐ a.m. ☐ p.m.	
Meal 6		**Meal 6**	
☐ a.m. ☐ p.m.		☐ a.m. ☐ p.m.	

Notes:

6.02

Body-*for*-LIFE

The 20-Minute Aerobics Solution™

Intensity Pattern

	PLAN		ACTUAL	
	Planned Start Time: _____		Actual Start Time: Y:50	
	Planned End Time: _____		Actual End Time: 8:18	
	Time to Complete: 20 Minutes		Time to Complete: _____	
Exercise	Minute by Minute	Intensity Level	Minute by Minute	Intensity Level
P3	1	5	1	5
	2	5	2	6
	3	6	3	7
	4	7	4	8
	5	8	5	9
	6	9	6	
	7	6	7	5
	8	7	8	6
	9	8	9	7
	10	9	10	8
	11	6	11	9
	12	7	12	
	13	8	13	5
	14	9	14	6
	15	6	15	7
	16	7	16	
	17	8	17	8
High Point	18	9	18	9
	19	10	19	9½
	20	5	20	5

Notes:

6.02   334

167.5

Bill Phillips   Lesson-*for*-LIFE

"A strong nation is made up of strong people."

America is literally a nation in crisis—inflating bodyfat levels and deflating economic strength. Each year, the United States government spends over $100 billion caring for Americans who didn't take care of themselves. That money goes to treat people who are suffering from obesity and its secondary diseases, such as diabetes, heart disease, vascular disease, cancer, etc. A lack of physical strength also contributes to millions of unnecessary injuries each year, which costs billions of dollars in lost productivity as well as medical bills. These very serious health issues can be prevented, in many cases, by following a program of regular exercise and proper nutrition like Body-*for*-LIFE. From a fiscal standpoint alone, you can see how vitally important it is to make sure we don't become a burden to our country, especially in this day and age. This is yet another reason we should all prioritize caring for our health.

Success Story   Jeffry Life, M.D.

Age 60•Meshoppen, PA•Physician
Reduced Bodyfat from 25% to 8%

After I went through a traumatic divorce, my self-esteem had never been lower, my waist never bigger, nor my cholesterol level higher. One of my patients showed me the Program. I realized it was time for a change. My results were remarkable. My cholesterol went from dangerously high levels to healthy levels. My energy level increased, and my medical practice has never been better. Today I teach my patients to take care of their health and to prevent illness through better nutrition and exercise. And I lead by example.

Body-*for*-LIFE   The Power Mindset

Please write down 5 things you can do between now and this time tomorrow
that will help you move forward in the direction of your 12-week goals.

	PLAN	ACTUAL
1		
2		
3		
4		
5		

Body-*for*-LIFE   The Universal Law of Reciprocation

Please write down 2 things you can do between now and
this time tomorrow to support and encourage others.

	PLAN	ACTUAL
1		
2		

Body-*for*-LIFE   Focus on Progress, Not Perfection

Please write down 3 things you did very well today that helped
you move toward the achievement of your 12-week goals.

1	
2	
3	

Please write down one thing you will do even better tomorrow.

1	

Notes:

Body-*for*-LIFE   The Eating-*for*-LIFE Method™

PLAN		ACTUAL	
Meal 1		**Meal 1**	
☐ a.m. ☐ p.m.	mesotech	☐ a.m. ☐ p.m.	
Meal 2		**Meal 2**	
☐ a.m. ☐ p.m.	myoplex	☐ a.m. ☐ p.m.	
Meal 3		**Meal 3**	
☐ a.m. ☐ p.m.	Mrx	☐ a.m. ☐ p.m.	
Meal 4		**Meal 4**	
☐ a.m. ☐ p.m.	Mrx	☐ a.m. ☐ p.m.	
Meal 5		**Meal 5**	
☐ a.m. ☐ p.m.	Fun/rolen	☐ a.m. ☐ p.m.	
Meal 6		**Meal 6**	
☐ a.m. ☐ p.m.	Mesotec	☐ a.m. ☐ p.m.	

Notes:

Body-*for*-LIFE | Lower Body Workout

Intensity Pattern

	PLAN		ACTUAL
Planned Start Time: 7:15		Actual Start Time: ___	
Planned End Time: 7:59		Actual End Time: 31"	
Time to Complete: 42 Minutes		Time to Complete: ___	

Lower Body Muscle Groups	Exercise	Reps	Weight (lbs)	Minutes Between Sets	Intensity Level	Reps	Weight (lbs)	Minutes Between Sets	Intensity Level
Quads	2x1	12	120	1	5	12	125	1	5
		10	125	1	6	10	125	1	6
		8	125	1	7 2.34	8	125	1	7
		6	125	1	8 4"	6	125	1	8
High Point	squat	12	125	0	9 5.53	12	125	0	8
		12	90	2	10	12	80	2	2
Ham-strings	curls	12	60	1	5 1.39	12	60	1	5
		10	65	1	6	10"	65	1	6
		8	70	1	7	8 12"	70	1	9
		6	75	1	8	6 14.33	75	1	8
High Point	lunge	12	70	0	9	12 '	70	0	8
		12	40	2	10	12	40	-2	6
Calves	D.lift	12	40	1	5 20.47	12	40	1	5
		10	45	1	6 23.22	10	45	1	6
		8	45	1	7 24.50	8	45	1	7
		6	45	1	8 26.2	6	45	1	8
High Point	uni	12	45	0	9 29.48	12	45	0	9
		12	40	2	10	12	45	2	9
At this point, you should be 31 minutes into your lower body workout and have 11 minutes to go.									
Abs	reverse	12	0	1	5 31	12	0	1	5
		10	0	1	6	10	0	1	6
		8	0	1	7 34.2	8	0	1	7
		6	0	1	8	6	0	1	8
High Point	crunch	12	0	0	9	12	0	0	9
		12		–	10	12	0	0	2

Notes: Ø Δ in curls
lunge @ 40 → rep↑ nxt w/o

Bill Phillips Lesson-*for*-LIFE

"When you say no, you're also saying yes."

When you sit down and make plans for when you're going to work out, what you're going to eat, when you're going to eat, as well as decide what goals you're going to achieve each day, you're not only making a list of the things you *will* do, you're making a list of things you *won't* do. For example, if your friends invite you out for pizza and beer and it's not your free day, you have to just flat out say *no*. Saying no to people does not mean pushing them away or isolating yourself. It means that you're making changes for the better—changing your priorities, changing your habits, and changing your life. Realize that when you say no, you're also saying *yes*. You're saying yes to taking another step forward to looking and feeling better; you're saying yes to building your self-discipline, increasing your self-esteem, strengthening your willpower, and gaining control of your life!

Success Story Merrily Milmore

Age 48•Tiburon, CA• Health Practitioner
Decreased Bodyfat from 33% to 21%
Lost 28 lbs of Fat

Completing this Program helped me learn that a small amount of discipline can lead to an extraordinary amount of freedom. Freedom to be myself. Without my realizing it, my lack of attention to health and fitness began to imprison me. With 30 lbs of unwanted bodyfat, which I accumulated through a lack of discipline, I had imprisoned myself. I was stuck in a body I didn't like. And I was beginning to get stuck in a life I didn't love. I set myself free, not just one day at a time, but one disciplined decision at a time.

Body-*for*-LIFE — The Power Mindset

Please write down 5 things you can do between now and this time tomorrow that will help you move forward in the direction of your 12-week goals.

	PLAN	ACTUAL
1		
2		
3		
4		
5		

Body-*for*-LIFE — The Universal Law of Reciprocation

Please write down 2 things you can do between now and this time tomorrow to support and encourage others.

	PLAN	ACTUAL
1		
2		

Body-*for*-LIFE — Focus on Progress, Not Perfection

Please write down 3 things you did very well today that helped you move toward the achievement of your 12-week goals.

1	
2	
3	

Please write down one thing you will do even better tomorrow.

1	

Notes:

Body-*for*-LIFE | The Eating-*for*-LIFE Method™

PLAN			ACTUAL		
Meal 1			**Meal 1**		
☐ a.m. ☐ p.m.	mesotech		☐ a.m. ☐ p.m.		
Meal 2			**Meal 2**		
☐ a.m. ☐ p.m.	MTrx		☐ a.m. ☐ p.m.		
Meal 3			**Meal 3**		
☐ a.m. ☐ p.m.	$\frac{1}{2}$ Turky		☐ a.m. ☐ p.m.		
Meal 4			**Meal 4**		
☐ a.m. ☐ p.m.	$\frac{1}{2}$ Turh		☐ a.m. ☐ p.m.		
Meal 5			**Meal 5**		
☐ a.m. ☐ p.m.	myoplex		☐ a.m. ☐ p.m.		
Meal 6			**Meal 6**		
☐ a.m. ☐ p.m.	fish/salan		☐ a.m. ☐ p.m.		

Notes: 2 thermogenic
Rx

Body for-LIFE — The 20-Minute Aerobics Solution™

Intensity Pattern

Exercise	PLAN Minute by Minute	PLAN Intensity Level	ACTUAL Minute by Minute	ACTUAL Intensity Level
	1	5	1	5
	2	5	2	6
	3	6	3	7
	4	7	4	
	5	8	5	8
P3	6	9	6	9
	7	6	7	
level 3	8	7	8	5
	9	8	9	6
	10	9	10	7
	11	6	11	8
	12	7	12	9
	13	8	13	5
	14	9	14	6
	15	6	15	7
	16	7	16	8
	17	8	17	9
High Point	18	9	18	
	19	10	19	5½
	20	5	20	5

PLAN — Planned Start Time: ___ Planned End Time: ___ Time to Complete: 20 Minutes
ACTUAL — Actual Start Time: ___ Actual End Time: ___ Time to Complete: ___

Notes: 6.04 km
325 cal
183 — 165
try level 4
Saturday

Bill Phillips — Lesson-*for*-LIFE

"Winners finish, and finishers win."

Thousands of people who decide to complete the Body-*for*-LIFE Program are competing in the official EAS Challenge, where big cash prizes, dream vacations, and other material incentives are the reward. Competing in the EAS Challenge can increase focus while also making the process more fun. However, I want to point out that you *don't* have to be selected as a Champion in the EAS competition to be a *winner*. In my opinion, anyone and everyone who finishes the 12-week Program is a winner! As I see it, a winner is someone who accepts challenges and sees them through from start to finish. A winner is someone who reaches higher and finds the strength and courage to accomplish important goals. When you finish this Program, you will discover the true grand prize is the new body and life you've created. You are just 18 days away from that breakthrough experience!

Success Story — Tony Chaney

Age 30 • Bluffton, IN • Manager
Gained 29 lbs of Muscle

In high school, I joined the wrestling team. Halfway through the season, I hadn't had much success and I quit. Dad told me that no one wins all the time, but the real champion is the one who can get his butt kicked and be better because of it, not in spite of it. He taught me to never give up and always look for lessons to be learned. So I stayed on the team and kept trying and winning. That's how I finished the Body-*for*-LIFE Program. I learned from every mistake and never gave up! I give my dad credit for my transformation.

Body-*for*-LIFE   The Power Mindset

Please write down 5 things you can do between now and this time tomorrow
that will help you move forward in the direction of your 12-week goals.

	PLAN	ACTUAL
1		
2		
3		
4		
5		

Body-*for*-LIFE   The Universal Law of Reciprocation

Please write down 2 things you can do between now and
this time tomorrow to support and encourage others.

	PLAN	ACTUAL
1		
2		

Body-*for*-LIFE   Focus on Progress, Not Perfection

Please write down 3 things you did very well today that helped
you move toward the achievement of your 12-week goals.

1	
2	
3	

Please write down one thing you will do even better tomorrow.

1	

Notes:

DAY 66

Body-*for*-LIFE The Eating-*for*-LIFE Method™

PLAN		ACTUAL	
Meal 1		**Meal 1**	
☐ a.m. ☐ p.m.	menker	☐ a.m. ☐ p.m.	Mtx
Meal 2		**Meal 2**	
☐ a.m. ☐ p.m.	Mtx	☐ a.m. ☐ p.m.	
Meal 3		**Meal 3**	
☐ a.m. ☐ p.m.	myuph,	☐ a.m. ☐ p.m.	
Meal 4		**Meal 4**	
☐ a.m. ☐ p.m.	myupts	☐ a.m. ☐ p.m.	myupts Da
Meal 5		**Meal 5**	
☐ a.m. ☐ p.m.	Fish juicen	☐ a.m. ☐ p.m.	salmon + perts
Meal 6		**Meal 6**	
☐ a.m. ☐ p.m.	menten	☐ a.m. ☐ p.m.	

Notes: w7 166

Body-*for*-LIFE | Upper Body Workout

Intensity Pattern

	PLAN	ACTUAL
Planned Start Time: 6:30	Actual Start Time: 9:0
Planned End Time: 7:16	Actual End Time: 7:46
Time to Complete: 46 Minutes	Time to Complete: 4r

Upper Body Muscle Groups	Exercise	Reps	Weight (lbs)	Minutes Between Sets	Intensity Level	Reps	Weight (lbs)	Minutes Between Sets	Intensity Level
Chest	incline	12	40	1	5	12	148	1	5
	BP	10	45	1	6	10	84r	1	6
		8	45	1	7 2·1 8	8	14r	1	7
		6	45	1	8 24	6	14r	1	8
High Point		12	45	0	9 0.4r	12	4r	0	9
	flyer	12	35	2	10	12	3r	2	9
Shoulders	military	12	25	1	5 7.3r	12	25	1	5
	press	10	30	1	6 14.21	10	30	1	6
		8	35	1	7 12.5u	8	3r	1	7
		6	40	1	8 17	6	40	1	8
High Point		12	35	0	9 15.1r	12	3r	0	8
	lat rair	12	10	2	10	12	10	2	
Back	rowr	12	40	1	5 19.0	12	·0	1	6
		10	45	1	6 20	10	45	1	6
		8	45	1	7 21.4	8	4r	1	7
		6	45	1	8 23.0	6	4r	1	8
High Point		12	45	0	9 24.2r	12	4r	0	8
	2 arm	12	30	2	10	12	30	2	8
Triceps	c x7	12	25	1	5 27.3	12	25	1	1
		10	25	1	6 29.0	10	2r	1	6
		8	25	1	7 30.50	8	2r	1	7
		6	25	1	8 32.41	6	2r	1	8
High Point		12	25	0	9	12	25	0	8
	airi	12	0	2	10	12 ✓	0	2	8

At this point, you should be 37 minutes into your upper body workout and have 9 minutes to go.

Biceps	curl	12	20	1	5 38.1	12	20	1	5
		10	25	1	6 30.4	10	25	1	6
		8	30	1	7 40.2	8	30	1	7
		6	35	1	8 41.7	6	3r	1	8
High Point		12	30	0	9 43.0	12	30	0	8
		12	25	–	10	12		2	

Notes:

Bill Phillips — Lesson-*for*-LIFE

> "The more we follow our hearts,
> the more success we experience."

I have a puppy named T-Rex (short for Tinysaurus Rex). He's a little Yorkshire terrier. He has so much positive energy. He is so happy. His life is very simple: He wakes up, eats, plays, eats, sleeps, and plays. He is open, affectionate, and loving with everyone he meets. He's perfect just the way he is because he follows his instincts. I love that about animals. And although human beings have been blessed, *and* cursed, with minds that are much more complicated, I can't help but notice that the more we do what comes naturally—the more we *follow our hearts*, our instincts, our intuitions—the more success we experience, the more aligned and balanced we become. We're more peaceful, healthier, and happier. As you continue on with this process, I encourage you to pay attention to that inner voice, that instinct, and follow it.

Success Story — Dianne Moylan

Age 45•Lakeland, FL•Author/Success Coach
Lost 17 lbs of Fat, Gained 2 lbs of Muscle
Reduced Cholesterol from 184 to 143

At first I worried that following Body-*for*-LIFE would turn too much of my focus on me. But the opposite happened. When I began to feel better and look healthier, it opened me up to other people. The way I connect with people is very different now. I see their confidence and trust in me. I feel their respect. This has deepened all my relationships, old and new. I feel more certainty, clarity, and purpose than I have in a long time. I feel more centered and more aware of my intuition as a result of this experience.

DAY 67

Body-*for*-LIFE   The Power Mindset

Please write down 5 things you can do between now and this time tomorrow that will help you move forward in the direction of your 12-week goals.

	PLAN	ACTUAL
1		
2		
3		
4		
5		

Body-*for*-LIFE   The Universal Law of Reciprocation

Please write down 2 things you can do between now and this time tomorrow to support and encourage others.

	PLAN	ACTUAL
1		
2		

Body-*for*-LIFE   Focus on Progress, Not Perfection

Please write down 3 things you did very well today that helped you move toward the achievement of your 12-week goals.

1	
2	
3	

Please write down one thing you will do even better tomorrow.

1	

Notes:

Body-*for*-LIFE The Eating-*for*-LIFE Method™

PLAN		ACTUAL	
Meal 1		**Meal 1**	
☑ a.m. ☐ p.m.	mrx	☐ a.m. ☐ p.m.	
Meal 2		**Meal 2**	
☐ a.m. ☐ p.m.	myspl	☐ a.m. ☐ p.m.	
Meal 3		**Meal 3**	
☐ a.m. ☐ p.m.	salan + tln	☐ a.m. ☐ p.m.	
Meal 4		**Meal 4**	
☐ a.m. ☐ p.m.	myspl	☐ a.m. ☐ p.m.	
Meal 5		**Meal 5**	
☐ a.m. ☐ p.m.	chln	☐ a.m. ☐ p.m.	
Meal 6		**Meal 6**	
☐ a.m. ☐ p.m.		☐ a.m. ☐ p.m.	

Notes: 2 Thomas agmr

Body-*for*-LIFE

The 20-Minute Aerobics Solution™

Intensity Pattern

	PLAN		ACTUAL	
	Planned Start Time: 6:15		Actual Start Time: 6:35	
	Planned End Time: 6:35		Actual End Time: 6:55	
	Time to Complete: 20 Minutes		Time to Complete: 20'	
Exercise	Minute by Minute	Intensity Level	Minute by Minute	Intensity Level
	1	5	1	5
	2	5	2	6
	3	6	3	7
	4	7	4	8
	5	8	5	9
	6	9	6	5
(P3)	7	6	7	6
	8	7	8	7
	9	8	9	8
	10	9	10	9
	11	6	11	
	12	7	12	5
	13	8	13	6
	14	9	14	7
	15	6	15	
	16	7	16	8
	17	8	17	8
High Point	18	9	18	9
	19	10	19	
	20	5	20	5

Notes: 5.72 k̄n

3.12

165 — 161 —slow start

not as

w? 166? intense

Bill Phillips — Lesson-*for*-LIFE

"The Internet connection—a powerful, uplifting, worldwide support network."

When I wrote Body-*for*-LIFE three years ago, I never imagined the Internet would have such an impact on the amount of good this book could do. But the fact is, the powerful ability of the Internet to connect people from all over the world and to empower them to communicate their ideas, share their experiences, and support one another has turned out to be a real advantage for people who, like you, have accepted this Challenge. Many people, from all over the world, have become leaders and are helping support people who have made the decision to improve their bodies and lives. I cannot thank these people enough. If you don't already participate in a Body-*for*-LIFE Internet community, I encourage you to do so. You can find an index of my favorite independent Body-*for*-LIFE online communities by visiting www.BodyforLIFE.com.

Success Story — Tracy and John Griffin

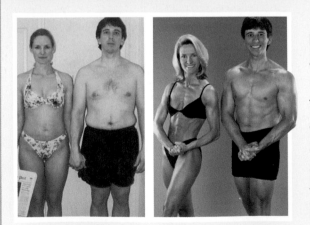

Ages 35 and 36•Sterling, VA
Housewife/Operations Manager
Tracy Lost 8 lbs of Bodyfat, Gained 3 lbs of Muscle
John Lost 16 lbs of Bodyfat, Gained 5 lbs of Muscle

During the Challenge, we realized how important support and encouragement was. When we needed inspiration, we were there for each other. The before and after photos of past champions, which we put on our walls and refrigerator, gave us support and encouragement too. If they could do it, then so could we! We have decided to make fitness a way of life for our family, and we encourage everyone we know to follow our example. The Challenge has completely changed the direction of our lives!

Body-*for*-LIFE   The Power Mindset

Please write down 5 things you can do between now and this time tomorrow
that will help you move forward in the direction of your 12-week goals.

PLAN	ACTUAL
1	
2	
3	
4	
5	

Body-*for*-LIFE   The Universal Law of Reciprocation

Please write down 2 things you can do between now and
this time tomorrow to support and encourage others.

PLAN	ACTUAL
1	
2	

Body-*for*-LIFE   Focus on Progress, Not Perfection

Please write down 3 things you did very well today that helped
you move toward the achievement of your 12-week goals.

1	
2	
3	

Please write down one thing you will do even better tomorrow.

1	

Notes:

Body-*for*-LIFE | The Eating-*for*-LIFE Method™

PLAN	ACTUAL

Meal 1

☐ a.m.
☐ p.m.

Menolect

Meal 1

☐ a.m.
☐ p.m.

Meal 2

☐ a.m.
☐ p.m.

rey optea
½ tuna

Meal 2

☐ a.m.
☐ p.m.

Meal 3

☐ a.m.
☐ p.m.

gitten
chkn.
salad

Meal 3

☐ a.m.
☐ p.m.

Meal 4

☐ a.m.
☐ p.m.

myoplx

Meal 4

☐ a.m.
☐ p.m.

Meal 5

☐ a.m.
☐ p.m.

Fish
1 chicks

Meal 5

☐ a.m.
☐ p.m.

Meal 6

☐ a.m.
☐ p.m.

Meal 6

☐ a.m.
☐ p.m.

Notes:

Body-*for*-LIFE   Lower Body Workout

	PLAN		ACTUAL

Intensity Pattern

PLAN

Planned Start Time: 6:15

Planned End Time: 7:00

Time to Complete: 42 Minutes

ACTUAL

Actual Start Time: 6:37

Actual End Time: _____

Time to Complete: 37"

Lower Body Muscle Groups	Exercise	Reps	Weight (lbs)	Minutes Between Sets	Intensity Level	Reps	Weight (lbs)	Minutes Between Sets	Intensity Level
Quads		12	120	1	5	12	120	1	5
	@ x7	10	125	1	6	10	121	1	6
		8	125	1	7	8 2.5 +2.5	125	1	7
		6	125	1	8	6	125	1	5
High Point	squat	12	125	0	9 5.59	12	125	c	9
		12	90	2	10	12	90	2	9
Hamstrings	curl	12	60	1	5 6.5	12	60	1	5
		10	65	1	6 11:35	10	65	1	6
		8	70	1	7	8 13:10 / 15"	70	1	7
		6	75	1	8	6	75	0	5
High Point		12	70	0	9 (5.49)	12	70	c	8
		12	40	2	10	12	40	2	
Calves		12	40	1	5 23	12	40	1	5
		10	45	1	6 24:40	10	45	1	6
		8	45	1	7 25:30	8	41	1	4
		6	45	1	8 27"	6	45	1	8
High Point		12	45	0	9	12	45	c	9
		12	35	2	10	12	35	2	8

At this point, you should be 31 minutes into your lower body workout and have 11 minutes to go.

Lower Body Muscle Groups	Exercise	Reps	Weight (lbs)	Minutes Between Sets	Intensity Level	Reps	Weight (lbs)	Minutes Between Sets	Intensity Level
Abs	reven	12	12	1	5 31	12	0	1	5
	crnch	10	10	1	6	10	0	1	6
		8	8	1	7	8	0	1	7
		6	6	1	8	6	0	1	8
High Point	bell crna	12	12	0	9	12		c	3
		12	12	–	10	12		2	7

Notes: _____ c little vern _____
_____ nomiting cud — dry by (5) na _____

DAY 69

Bill Phillips   Lesson-*for*-LIFE

"Your actions speak much louder than your words."

It's a misconception that only top athletes, actors, and public figures are "role models" or examples. The fact is, we're all an example of something... but what? Realize that your *actions* speak much louder than your words and those around you—family, friends, co-workers—are *always* listening. This is an especially important issue for parents as it's well established that children model your behavior and "inherit" your style of living; your good and bad habits are being passed on. How you eat, how you exercise, how much you support and encourage others, whether you set worthwhile goals and do what it takes to achieve your objectives—all that, and more. We all have an opportunity to be a positive example and a good role model to those around us. And through this Body-*for*-LIFE experience, you are becoming a positive example of how to live a healthier life. Good work!

Success Story   Tony Young

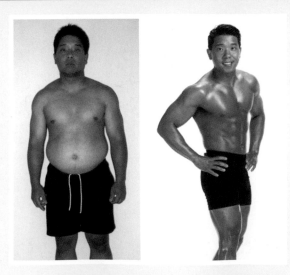

Age 32•Canyon Country, CA•Negotiator, JPL/NASA
Reduced Bodyfat from 29% to 14%

After seeing a photo of myself at a pool party last summer, I knew I needed to get back in shape. My young children were the biggest inspirations; they helped me stay on course throughout the Challenge. I wanted so badly to be a good role model for them to look up to in many aspects. I wanted them (especially my son, Brandon) to realize the importance of setting worthwhile goals and achieving them. I wanted to show him the discipline required to achieve success. Now he, too, wants to be healthy and strong like his dad!

DAY 69

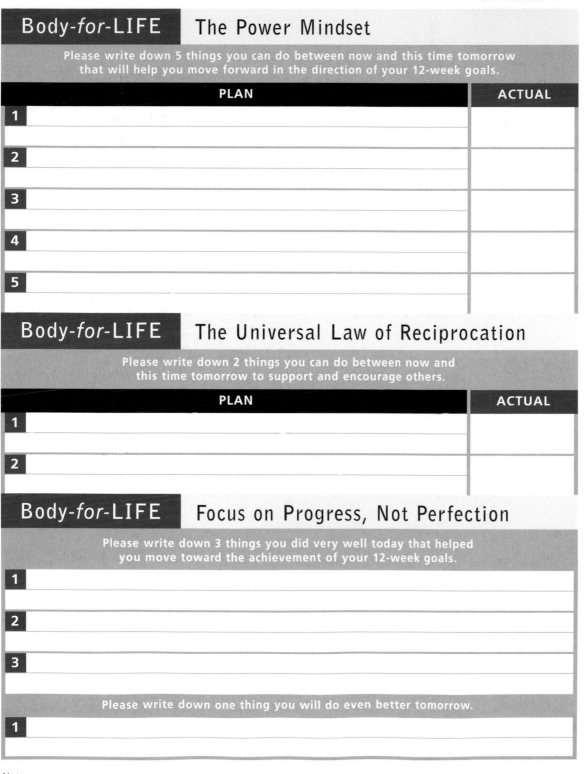

Body-*for*-LIFE The Power Mindset

Please write down 5 things you can do between now and this time tomorrow that will help you move forward in the direction of your 12-week goals.

	PLAN	ACTUAL
1		
2		
3		
4		
5		

Body-*for*-LIFE The Universal Law of Reciprocation

Please write down 2 things you can do between now and this time tomorrow to support and encourage others.

	PLAN	ACTUAL
1		
2		

Body-*for*-LIFE Focus on Progress, Not Perfection

Please write down 3 things you did very well today that helped you move toward the achievement of your 12-week goals.

1	
2	
3	

Please write down one thing you will do even better tomorrow.

1	

Notes:

DAY 69

Body-*for*-LIFE — The Eating-*for*-LIFE Method™

PLAN		ACTUAL	
Meal 1		**Meal 1**	
☐ a.m. ☐ p.m.	cuffo Fast far	☐ a.m. ☐ p.m.	from fred
Meal 2		**Meal 2**	
☐ a.m. ☐ p.m.		☐ a.m. ☐ p.m.	trisple
Meal 3		**Meal 3**	
☐ a.m. ☐ p.m.	salca + ocil	☐ a.m. ☐ p.m.	salch + m1
Meal 4		**Meal 4**	
☐ a.m. ☐ p.m.	myuphi vn	☐ a.m. ☐ p.m.	myophs urn
Meal 5		**Meal 5**	
☐ a.m. ☐ p.m.	salch + fish	☐ a.m. ☐ p.m.	-frsh fup -chup
Meal 6		**Meal 6**	
☐ a.m. ☐ p.m.		☐ a.m. ☐ p.m.	

Notes: — lon meal —rn n sin

DAY 69

Body-*for*-LIFE

The 20-Minute Aerobics Solution™

Intensity Pattern

	PLAN		ACTUAL	
	Planned Start Time: _____		Actual Start Time: 6.30	
	Planned End Time: _____		Actual End Time: 7.	
	Time to Complete: 20 Minutes		Time to Complete: 0~	
Exercise	Minute by Minute	Intensity Level	Minute by Minute	Intensity Level
	1	5	1	
	2	5	2	
	3	6	3	
	4	7	4	
5pmn	5	8	5	
	6	9	6	
20"	7	6	7	
	8	7	8	
level	9	8	9	
	10	9	10	
15"	11	6	11	
	12	7	12	
	13	8	13	
	14	9	14	
	15	6	15	
	16	7	16	
	17	8	17	
High Point	18	9	18	
	19	10	19	
	20	5	20	

Notes: clr/nn 3vrn f.1
r 3 v sc sln

ur | bl. r-

Bill Phillips — Lesson-*for*-LIFE

> "In a world of uncertainty, you are
> the one thing you can count on!"

These are uncertain times, there's no doubt about it—acts of terrorism, hijacked airliners, Fortune 500 companies going bankrupt, etc. It's no wonder people are experiencing more anxiety and stress as they feel things are getting out of control. And while it's true there are many things in this world that will never be within our control, there is a tremendous opportunity for empowerment by taking charge of the things you *can* control. Your health, your body, your mind… these have *always* been the center of your universe, and when you gain control over these aspects of your life, you will not only increase your physical and mental strength, you'll be able to help others cope in these troubled times. So, please, remember that in this world of uncertainty, which we all share, *you* are the one thing you *can* count on!

Success Story — Larry Patrick

Age 56•Edmond, OK•Developer
Gained 8 lbs of Muscle, Lost 42 lbs of Fat

It's been said that a person's happiness is directly proportionate to the amount of control they feel they have over their lives. Through Body-*for*-LIFE, I have gone from feeling out of control to being in control… and my happiness has changed accordingly. My advice to others is to accept the Challenge. Don't just *try* your best—*do* your best. Make every decision based on what will give you the best chance to succeed. The true measure of your success is how close you come to 100% of *your* capabilities.

Body-*for*-LIFE   The Power Mindset

Please write down 5 things you can do between now and this time tomorrow
that will help you move forward in the direction of your 12-week goals.

	PLAN	ACTUAL
1		
2		
3		
4		
5		

Body-*for*-LIFE   The Universal Law of Reciprocation

Please write down 2 things you can do between now and
this time tomorrow to support and encourage others.

	PLAN	ACTUAL
1		
2		

Body-*for*-LIFE   Focus on Progress, Not Perfection

Please write down 3 things you did very well today that helped
you move toward the achievement of your 12-week goals.

1	
2	
3	

Please write down one thing you will do even better tomorrow.

1	

Notes:

Body-*for*-LIFE   The Eating-*for*-LIFE Method™

PLAN	ACTUAL

Meal 1

☐ a.m.
☐ p.m.

Mesotech
moyoptex

Meal 1

☐ a.m.
☐ p.m.

Meal 2

☐ a.m.
☐ p.m.

myoplex

Meal 2

☐ a.m.
☐ p.m.

Meal 3

☐ a.m.
☐ p.m.

tuni

Meal 3

☐ a.m.
☐ p.m.

Meal 4

☐ a.m.
☐ p.m.

tuna

Meal 4

☐ a.m.
☐ p.m.

Meal 5

☐ a.m.
☐ p.m.

salad
fish/stin

Meal 5

☐ a.m.
☐ p.m.

Meal 6

☐ a.m.
☐ p.m.

MTX

Meal 6

☐ a.m.
☐ p.m.

Notes:

Body-*for*-LIFE — Upper Body Workout

		PLAN				ACTUAL			

Intensity Pattern

PLAN
Planned Start Time: _____
Planned End Time: _____
Time to Complete: 46 Minutes

ACTUAL
Actual Start Time: 8:53
Actual End Time: _____
Time to Complete: _____

Upper Body Muscle Groups	Exercise	Reps	Weight (lbs)	Minutes Between Sets	Intensity Level	Reps	Weight (lbs)	Minutes Between Sets	Intensity Level
Chest	incline BP	12	40	1	5	12	40	1	5
		10	45	1	6	10	45	1	6
		8	45	1	7 2.21	8	45	1	7
		6	45	1	8 3.55	6	45	1	
High Point	flyer	12	45	0	9 5.25	12	45	0	
		12	35	2	10	12	35	0	
Shoulders	military	12	25	1	5 8 8	12	25	1	5
	pres	10	30	1	6 4.2	10	33	1	6
		8	35	1	7 11.8	8	35	1	7
		6	40	1	8	6	40-3	1	8
High Point	leg rain	12	35	0	9 17.5	12	35	8	9
		12	12	2	10	12		2	9
Back	rows	12	40	1	5 N 8	12	40	1	5
		10	45	1	6 20.53	10	45	1	6
		8	45	1	7 20.53	8	45	1	7
		6	45	1	8 22.1	6	45	1	5
High Point		12	45	0	9 23.3	12	45	0	9
		12	40	2	10	12	40	2	9
Triceps	ec	12	25	1	5	24	25	1	5
		10		1	6 8.8	10	25	1	6
		8		1	7	8	25	1	4
		6		1	8	6	25	1	8
High Point	air	12		0	9	12	25	0	8
		12	12	2	10	12		2	3

At this point, you should be 37 minutes into your upper body workout and have 9 minutes to go.

		Reps	Weight (lbs)	Minutes Between Sets	Intensity Level	Reps	Weight (lbs)	Minutes Between Sets	Intensity Level
Biceps	curls	12	20	1	5	12	20	1	5
		10	25	1	6	10	25	1	6
		8	30	1	7	8	30	1	7
		6	35	1	8	6	31	1	8
High Point		12	35	0	9	12	25	0	9
	ncmnc cup	12	35	–	10	12	25	1	9

Notes:

Bill Phillips — Lesson-*for*-LIFE

> "Learning something new is always
> hard before it's easy."

When we begin to learn and venture into new territory is when we have the opportunity to experience significant growth. No matter what it is, if you're just learning it, you're going to be awkward at first. This is true of exercising, learning to ride a bicycle, dancing, golfing, giving a speech, etc. You must be willing to go through the "novice stage" if you want to ever become an expert. During this Program, it's very likely you've had to learn new skills. You may have needed to learn new exercises. It's likely you needed to learn how to prepare meals in a new way, and how to use the Plan-to-Actual Analysis in this *Success Journal*. But, you *are* doing it! I encourage you to be empowered by this experience and to give yourself permission to be a beginner—a learner—in other areas of your life, so you continue to evolve and improve!

Success Story — Tiffany Gatesh

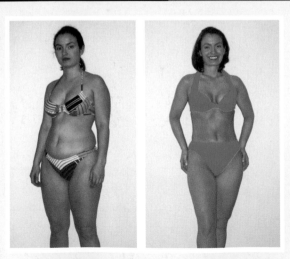

Age 34•Chatham, NJ•Mother/Law Student
Gained Energy, Lost 19 lbs of Fat
Reduced Dress Size from Size 8 to Size 2

I've always been goal-oriented, but in the past year I was stagnant. Then I realized by reading past success stories that *unless* you try to do something beyond what you have already mastered, you will never grow. I accepted this Challenge, knowing I had no idea how to even go about doing it. By following the Body-*for*-LIFE Program to the letter, I learned, week by week, how to transform. I never thought I would be an expert on the High Point Technique, proper nutrition, and how to set daily fitness goals! But, now I am!

Body-*for*-LIFE — The Power Mindset

Please write down 5 things you can do between now and this time tomorrow that will help you move forward in the direction of your 12-week goals.

	PLAN	ACTUAL
1		
2		
3		
4		
5		

Body-*for*-LIFE — The Universal Law of Reciprocation

Please write down 2 things you can do between now and this time tomorrow to support and encourage others.

	PLAN	ACTUAL
1		
2		

Body-*for*-LIFE — Focus on Progress, Not Perfection

Please write down 3 things you did very well today that helped you move toward the achievement of your 12-week goals.

1	
2	
3	

Please write down one thing you will do even better tomorrow.

1	

Notes:

DAY 72

Body-*for*-LIFE The Eating-*for*-LIFE Method™

PLAN		ACTUAL	
Meal 1		**Meal 1**	
☑ a.m. ☐ p.m. 8:00	mesotech	☐ a.m. ☐ p.m. 9:00	myoplex orisnl
Meal 2		**Meal 2**	
☐ a.m. ☐ p.m.	MTrx	☐ a.m. ☐ p.m.	MTrx
Meal 3		**Meal 3**	
☐ a.m. ☐ p.m.	tunc	☐ a.m. ☐ p.m.	tuna
Meal 4		**Meal 4**	
☐ a.m. ☐ p.m.	tvnn	☐ a.m. ☐ p.m.	selmm
Meal 5		**Meal 5**	
☐ a.m. ☐ p.m.	½ strn crphnn	☐ a.m. ☐ p.m.	salsa selmon Tsn
Meal 6		**Meal 6**	
☐ a.m. ☐ p.m.	myoplx	☐ a.m. ☐ p.m.	

Notes:

Body-*for*-LIFE

The 20-Minute Aerobics Solution™

Intensity Pattern

Exercise	PLAN		ACTUAL	
	Planned Start Time: 6:30		**Actual Start Time:** 7:30	
	Planned End Time: 6:50		**Actual End Time:** 7:50	
	Time to Complete: 20 Minutes		**Time to Complete:** 20	
	Minute by Minute	Intensity Level	Minute by Minute	Intensity Level
	1	5	1	5
	2	5	2	5
	3	6	3	6
	4	7	4	7
	5	8	5	8
	6	9	6	9
	7	6	7	
	8	7	8	5
	9	8	9	6
	10	9	10	7
	11	6	11	8
	12	7	12	
	13	8	13	9
	14	9	14	5
	15	6	15	6
	16	7	16	7
	17	8	17	8
High Point	18	9	18	9
	19	10	19	8
	20	5	20	5

P3

level

⑤

2 mins

Notes:

5.68 km

303 A

175

↓ — curl our m

168

↓ — 2m

141

Bill Phillips — Lesson-*for*-LIFE

"Feed your body and mind the right way."

Certainly, to lose bodyfat and to strengthen your muscles, you need to feed your body the right way—to nourish it with quality foods. Likewise, you need to *feed your mind* the right way to experience a successful transformation. To make it through this 12-week Program, and do so in championship style, you're going to need enthusiasm, optimism, and positive energy. And you can't just expect those things to come your way by accident. You need to intentionally feed your mind with positive, uplifting ideas, thoughts, and images. Among the ways to feed your mind healthily is by reading empowering books and investing time talking with winners: people who, like you, are dedicated to doing something positive with their lives. Today and every day, make a conscious effort to look for what's right in people, including yourself, and you'll find more good food for positive thought!

Success Story — Lynn Lingenfelter

Age 32 • Orangeville, PA • Author/Speaker
Gained Muscle While Losing 13% Bodyfat

During your voyage through life, you're going to hit adversity—a storm. And even though things might get very rough, you should never stop going forward. Never give up. If you drop anchor, the storm will tear you apart. Look forward, and you will see the beautiful rainbow on the other side. Keep looking forward and move in that direction, and you will make it through. And try to make the most of every day, starting now—live as you will wish you would have lived when you're dying!

Body-*for*-LIFE   The Power Mindset

Please write down 5 things you can do between now and this time tomorrow
that will help you move forward in the direction of your 12-week goals.

	PLAN	ACTUAL
1		
2		
3		
4		
5		

Body-*for*-LIFE   The Universal Law of Reciprocation

Please write down 2 things you can do between now and
this time tomorrow to support and encourage others.

	PLAN	ACTUAL
1		
2		

Body-*for*-LIFE   Focus on Progress, Not Perfection

Please write down 3 things you did very well today that helped
you move toward the achievement of your 12-week goals.

1	
2	
3	

Please write down one thing you will do even better tomorrow.

1	

Notes:

DAY **73**

Body-*for*-LIFE   The Eating-*for*-LIFE Method™

PLAN		ACTUAL	
Meal 1		**Meal 1**	
☐ a.m. ☐ p.m.		☐ a.m. ☐ p.m.	
Meal 2		**Meal 2**	
☐ a.m. ☐ p.m.		☐ a.m. ☐ p.m.	
Meal 3		**Meal 3**	
☐ a.m. ☐ p.m.		☐ a.m. ☐ p.m.	
Meal 4		**Meal 4**	
☐ a.m. ☐ p.m.		☐ a.m. ☐ p.m.	
Meal 5		**Meal 5**	
☐ a.m. ☐ p.m.		☐ a.m. ☐ p.m.	
Meal 6		**Meal 6**	
☐ a.m. ☐ p.m.		☐ a.m. ☐ p.m.	

Notes:

Body-*for*-LIFE — Lower Body Workout

Intensity Pattern

	PLAN	ACTUAL
	Planned Start Time: 6:30	Actual Start Time: _____
	Planned End Time: 7:12	Actual End Time: _____
	Time to Complete: 42 Minutes	Time to Complete: _____

Lower Body Muscle Groups	Exercise	Reps	Weight (lbs)	Minutes Between Sets	Intensity Level	Reps	Weight (lbs)	Minutes Between Sets	Intensity Level
Quads	ex7	12	120	1	5	12	120	1	5
		10	125	1	6	10	125	1	6
		8	125	1	7	8 235	125	1	7
		6	125	1	8	6 4,13	125	1	8
High Point	squat	12	125	0	9	12	125	0	9
		12	90	2	10	12	90	2	8
Hamstrings	curl	12	60	1	5 9.31	12	60	1	5
		10	65	1	6 11,	10	65	1	6
		8	70	1	7	8	70	1	7
		6	75	1	8 14,2	6	75	1	8
High Point	lunge	12	70	0	9 16.0	12	70	0	9
		12	40	2	10	12	40	2	9
Calves	ex7	12	40	1	5 22.1	12	40	1	5
		10	45	1	6 2312	18	45	1	6
		8	45	1	7 2516	8	45	1	7
		6	45	1	8 26 46	6	45	1	8
High Point	cal	12	45	0	9	12	45	0	9
		12	85	2	10	12	40	2	

At this point, you should be 31 minutes into your lower body workout and have 11 minutes to go.

Abs	reven	12	0	1	5	12	0	1	5
		10	0	1	6	10	0	1	6
		8	0	1	7	8	0	1	7
		6	0	1	8	6	0	1	9
High Point	ball	12		0	9	12		0	9
		12		–	10	12		2	9

Notes:

Bill Phillips — Lesson-*for*-LIFE

"The end is a new beginning."

More and more people are discovering that when they end one 12-week Program, what feels *right* is for them to begin again—to set new goals and to continue their journey. For example, Mina Hobby completed four 12-week Programs and totally transformed her body and life! Her example is a tremendous inspiration for us all!

Success Story — Mina Hobby

Age 46 • Koloa, HI • Business Owner • Totally Transformed!

Being overweight was a lifelong problem for me. I struggled with an eating disorder that made dieting difficult. I looked "happy" on the outside, but inside I was hurting. I knew I needed to change and had tried many times. On January 1, 2000, I started Body-*for*-LIFE. I took my before photo. Ouch! At a height of 5'1" I weighed 200 lbs. I had a long way to go, but I stuck with it one day at a time. Weight lifting and aerobic workouts; Myoplex™ nutrition shakes and healthy foods and water; setting goals, planning, keeping a journal... I worked hard to do all these new things. And then the willpower paid off: People started encouraging and complimenting me! That inspired me to keep going! I completed four consecutive 12-week challenges and I lost 85 lbs! I have a level of energy, self-confidence, and personal strength that I never knew existed in me. And I'm now sharing that with others who, like me, have struggled with obesity.

Body-*for*-LIFE The Power Mindset

Please write down 5 things you can do between now and this time tomorrow that will help you move forward in the direction of your 12-week goals.

	PLAN	ACTUAL
1		
2		
3		
4		
5		

Body-*for*-LIFE The Universal Law of Reciprocation

Please write down 2 things you can do between now and this time tomorrow to support and encourage others.

	PLAN	ACTUAL
1		
2		

Body-*for*-LIFE Focus on Progress, Not Perfection

Please write down 3 things you did very well today that helped you move toward the achievement of your 12-week goals.

1	
2	
3	

Please write down one thing you will do even better tomorrow.

1	

Notes:

DAY 74

Body-*for*-LIFE The Eating-*for*-LIFE Method™

PLAN		ACTUAL	
Meal 1		**Meal 1**	
☐ a.m. ☐ p.m.	mesotech	☐ a.m. ☐ p.m.	promax
Meal 2		**Meal 2**	
☐ a.m. ☐ p.m.	myoptrs	☐ a.m. ☐ p.m.	myoplex
Meal 3		**Meal 3**	
☐ a.m. ☐ p.m.	tuns	☐ a.m. ☐ p.m.	tuna + clams + clms
Meal 4		**Meal 4**	
☐ a.m. ☐ p.m.	tuna	☐ a.m. ☐ p.m.	tuna + cm
Meal 5		**Meal 5**	
☐ a.m. ☐ p.m.	tuna + slns	☐ a.m. ☐ p.m.	tuna + slm + svnn
Meal 6		**Meal 6**	
☐ a.m. ☐ p.m.		☐ a.m. ☐ p.m.	

Notes:

Body-*for*-LIFE

Intensity Pattern

The 20-Minute Aerobics Solution™

	PLAN		ACTUAL	
	Planned Start Time: _____		Actual Start Time: _____	
	Planned End Time: _____		Actual End Time: _____	
	Time to Complete: 20 Minutes		Time to Complete: _____	
Exercise	Minute by Minute	Intensity Level	Minute by Minute	Intensity Level
	1	5	1	
	2	5	2	
	3	6	3	
	4	7	4	
	5	8	5	
	6	9	6	
⌐ ⌐	7	6	7	
	8	7	8	
	9	8	9	
	10	9	10	
	11	6	11	
	12	7	12	
	13	8	13	
	14	9	14	
	15	6	15	
	16	7	16	
	17	8	17	
High Point	18	9	18	
	19	10	19	
	20	5	20	

Notes:

1665

33 + N()

5 ()

Bill Phillips   Lesson-*for*-LIFE

"Life is open to your interpretation."

I feel very fortunate to have grown up with optimistic parents. My mom loves people, and people love her because when she's around, the world simply looks better. She sees the good even in "bad" situations. An example: One time, years ago, she was driving my brother and me home from Little League football practice. We heard a loud "boom" and our little red Volkswagon started to shimmy and shake. Mom pulled over, we got out of the car, she looked at the tire, then down the road, and then at my brother, Shawn, and me. She said, "Kids, do you realize how lucky we are?! If that tire had blown out going around that turn up there, we might have had an accident." Shawn and I nodded our heads, "Yeah! We *are* lucky!" The lesson: Your perspective on the things that will happen to you throughout the course of this Program, and throughout life, is open to *your* interpretation. A healthy perspective helps you enjoy a healthy life.

Success Story   Paul Sullivan

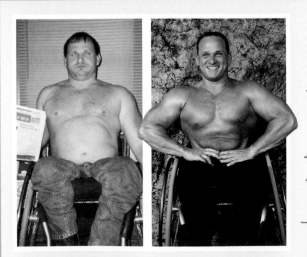

Age 45•Phelps, KY•Personal Trainer/Gym Owner
Completed Multiple 12-Week Programs
Gained Muscle, Lost Over 50 lbs of Fat

I accepted the Body-*for*-LIFE Challenge because I believe in leading by example. As a Success Coach and gym owner, I have helped 18 other people finish Body-*for*-LIFE with me. By coaching others, I have been inspired beyond words. This helped me see the good in myself and others. There's no better feeling. When I started the first Challenge three years ago, I weighed around 220. Now I weigh 170 with more muscle. If a man like me, confined to a wheelchair, can keep a positive outlook on life, why can't everyone?!

Body-*for*-LIFE   The Power Mindset

Please write down 5 things you can do between now and this time tomorrow that will help you move forward in the direction of your 12-week goals.

	PLAN	ACTUAL
1		
2		
3		
4		
5		

Body-*for*-LIFE   The Universal Law of Reciprocation

Please write down 2 things you can do between now and this time tomorrow to support and encourage others.

	PLAN	ACTUAL
1		
2		

Body-*for*-LIFE   Focus on Progress, Not Perfection

Please write down 3 things you did very well today that helped you move toward the achievement of your 12-week goals.

1	
2	
3	

Please write down one thing you will do even better tomorrow.

1	

Notes:

DAY 75

Body-*for*-LIFE — The Eating-*for*-LIFE Method™

PLAN		ACTUAL	
Meal 1		**Meal 1**	
☐ a.m. ☐ p.m.	MENKS	☐ a.m. ☐ p.m.	
Meal 2		**Meal 2**	
☐ a.m. ☐ p.m.	Mrx	☐ a.m. ☐ p.m.	
Meal 3		**Meal 3**	
☐ a.m. ☐ p.m.	CARB + salcd	☐ a.m. ☐ p.m.	
Meal 4		**Meal 4**	
☐ a.m. ☐ p.m.		☐ a.m. ☐ p.m.	
Meal 5		**Meal 5**	
☐ a.m. ☐ p.m.		☐ a.m. ☐ p.m.	
Meal 6		**Meal 6**	
☐ a.m. ☐ p.m.		☐ a.m. ☐ p.m.	

Notes:

Body-*for*-LIFE — Upper Body Workout

Intensity Pattern

	PLAN	ACTUAL
Planned Start Time: 6:00	Actual Start Time:
Planned End Time: 6:46	Actual End Time:
Time to Complete: 46 Minutes	Time to Complete:

Upper Body Muscle Groups	Exercise	Reps	Weight (lbs)	Minutes Between Sets	Intensity Level	Reps	Weight (lbs)	Minutes Between Sets	Intensity Level
Chest	*incln*	12	40	1	5	12	40	1	5
	BI	10	45	1	6	10	45	1	6
		8	45	1	7 2:11	8	45	1	7
		6	45	1	8 4.20	6	45	1	8
High Point	*F7*	12	45	0	9	12	45	0	8
		12	40	2	10	12	40	2	5
Shoulders	*r.l*	12	25	1	5 10.2	12	28	1	1
	r.r	10	30	1	6	10	30	1	1
		8	35	1	7 B2.14	8	35	1	1
		6	40	1	8	6	40	1	1
High Point	*17 r/r*	12	35	0	9	12	12	0	0
		12	10	2	10	12	12	2	2
Back	*rows*	12	40	1	5 21	12	40	1	5
		10	45	1	6 22.24	10	45	1	6
		8	45	1	7	8	45	1	7
		6	45	1	8 25.30	6	40	1	8
High Point	*pry*	12	45	0	9 29:11	12	45	0	9
		12	40	2	10	12	45	2	8
Triceps	*2 7*	12	25	1	5 30.8	12	25		
		10	25	1	6	10	25		
		8	25	1	7 33:30	8	25		
		6	25	1	8	6	28		
High Point	*cl.r*	12	25	0	9	12	25		
		12	12	2	10	12	—		

At this point, you should be 37 minutes into your upper body workout and have 9 minutes to go.

Upper Body Muscle Groups	Exercise	Reps	Weight (lbs)	Minutes Between Sets	Intensity Level	Reps	Weight (lbs)	Minutes Between Sets	Intensity Level
Biceps	*curls*	12	20	1	5	12	20		
		10	25	1	6 39.5	10	25		
		8	30	1	7 42.2	8	30		
		6	31	1	8	6	35		
High Point	*ncmm.cls*	12	30	0	9 (.4)	12	3		
		12	25	—	10	12			

Notes:

Bill Phillips — Lesson-*for*-LIFE

> "It's about being better than you used to be,
> not about being better than anyone else."

Succeeding with Body-*for*-LIFE is about becoming better than *you* used to be. It's not about being better than anyone else. It's about competing with yourself, not against someone else. It's about looking and feeling like a healthier version of you. It's about expressing who *you* really are and becoming even more of the unique, special person you were born to be. It's about building *your* best body. It's *not* about building a body like Cindy Crawford, Janet Jackson, Arnold, or Sly. And it's not about proving you have more willpower or discipline than others. It's about making the most out of what *you* have to work with. And the fact is, you *do* look and feel better right *now* than you did before Body-*for*-LIFE. And 8 days from now, when you finish this 12-week Program, you will look and feel even better! As I see it, that's success!

Success Story — India Venkitachalam

Age 53•Acton, MA•Business Owner
Gained 6 lbs of Muscle, Lost 14 lbs of Fat

My before photo shows a very sad face. It's the look of a woman who knew she was eating poorly and knew she was not caring for herself. But now, my reflection is of an extremely happy woman—the woman I had the potential to be all of this time. By accepting the Challenge and sticking with it, through thick and thin, I changed my body and my emotional health! I now am very proud to show my before and after photos to encourage others to take control and feel the joy of becoming better and better!

Body-*for*-LIFE The Power Mindset

Please write down 5 things you can do between now and this time tomorrow that will help you move forward in the direction of your 12-week goals.

	PLAN	ACTUAL
1		
2		
3		
4		
5		

Body-*for*-LIFE The Universal Law of Reciprocation

Please write down 2 things you can do between now and this time tomorrow to support and encourage others.

	PLAN	ACTUAL
1		
2		

Body-*for*-LIFE Focus on Progress, Not Perfection

Please write down 3 things you did very well today that helped you move toward the achievement of your 12-week goals.

1	
2	
3	

Please write down one thing you will do even better tomorrow.

1	

Notes:

Body-*for*-LIFE The Eating-*for*-LIFE Method™

PLAN	ACTUAL
Meal 1 ☐ a.m. ☐ p.m.	**Meal 1** ☐ a.m. ☐ p.m. *myplex*
Meal 2 ☐ a.m. ☐ p.m.	**Meal 2** ☐ a.m. *fruit* ☐ p.m.
Meal 3 ☐ a.m. ☐ p.m.	**Meal 3** ☐ a.m. *turkey* ☐ p.m. *+ salad*
Meal 4 ☐ a.m. ☐ p.m.	**Meal 4** ☐ a.m. *myoplex* ☐ p.m.
Meal 5 ☐ a.m. ☐ p.m.	**Meal 5** ☐ a.m. *Bar* ☐ p.m.
Meal 6 ☐ a.m. ☐ p.m.	**Meal 6** ☐ a.m. *turkey* ☐ p.m.

Notes:

Body-*for*-LIFE

The 20-Minute Aerobics Solution™

Intensity Pattern

	PLAN		ACTUAL	
Planned Start Time: _6:00_			Actual Start Time: _6:30_	
Planned End Time: _x20_			Actual End Time: _6,50_	
Time to Complete: 20 Minutes			Time to Complete: _____	

Exercise	Minute by Minute	Intensity Level	Minute by Minute	Intensity Level
	1	5	1	5
	2	5	2	
	3	6	3	
	4	7	4	
recumbent	5	8	5	
	6	9	6	
level	7	6	7	
20	8	7	8	hill
	9	8	9	interval
x20"	10	9	10	x20"
	11	6	11	
	12	7	12	
	13	8	13	
	14	9	14	
	15	6	15	
	16	7	16	
	17	8	17	
High Point	18	9	18	
	19	10	19	
	20	5	20	

Notes:

283 4 1   71n (187)

Bill Phillips — Lesson-*for*-LIFE

"Almost finished is <u>not</u> the same as finished."

Here we go! This is the <u>*first*</u> day of your *last* week of this 12-week Body-*for*-LIFE Program. The finish line is in sight, but please do not let up now—do *not* coast across the finish line. I want you to sprint! Make these last six workouts your absolute best ever! Hit your *highest* high points each and every day. Keep in mind that all the training you've done over the past 11 weeks has given you the increased endurance, energy, and inner strength to push yourself to new heights. This is your "high-point week," and it should be your most focused, most intense, and most successful of the entire 12-week Program. *This* is the time to push yourself harder than ever! Six days from now, when you take your after photo and make your final measurements, you'll be glad you gave this week your absolute best, and then some!

Success Story — Michael Lebsack

**Age 32•Juneau, AK•U.S. Coast Guard Officer
Lost 20 lbs of Fat, Gained Energy**

Before Body-*for*-LIFE, my lifestyle was not working for me; it was working against me. I was gaining bodyfat and becoming physically exhausted, which left me feeling frustrated, even angry. By accepting responsibility for my circumstances, taking control, making the decision to make a change, and completing the Program all the way from start to finish, I have become an upbeat, confident man whose company people really enjoy. This experience has empowered me and has literally changed my course in life.

Body-*for*-LIFE   The Power Mindset

Please write down 5 things you can do between now and this time tomorrow
that will help you move forward in the direction of your 12-week goals.

PLAN	ACTUAL
1	
2	
3	
4	
5	

Body-*for*-LIFE   The Universal Law of Reciprocation

Please write down 2 things you can do between now and
this time tomorrow to support and encourage others.

PLAN	ACTUAL
1	
2	

Body-*for*-LIFE   Focus on Progress, Not Perfection

Please write down 3 things you did very well today that helped
you move toward the achievement of your 12-week goals.

1	
2	
3	

Please write down one thing you will do even better tomorrow.

1	

Notes:

Body-*for*-LIFE   The Eating-*for*-LIFE Method™

PLAN	ACTUAL

Meal 1

☐ a.m.
☐ p.m.

Meal 1

☐ a.m.   mysptx
☐ p.m.

Meal 2

☐ a.m.
☐ p.m.

Meal 2

☐ a.m.   Mra
☐ p.m.

Meal 3

☐ a.m.
☐ p.m.

Meal 3

☐ a.m.   tum
☐ p.m.

Meal 4

☐ a.m.
☐ p.m.

Meal 4

☐ a.m.   tum
☐ p.m.

Meal 5

☐ a.m.
☐ p.m.

Meal 5

☐ a.m.   mysp14
☐ p.m.

Meal 6

☐ a.m.
☐ p.m.

Meal 6

☐ a.m.   MIre
☐ p.m.

Notes:

DAY 78

Body-*for*-LIFE — Lower Body Workout

Intensity Pattern

	PLAN		ACTUAL	
	Planned Start Time: 8:15		Actual Start Time:	
	Planned End Time: 8:57		Actual End Time:	
	Time to Complete: 42 Minutes		Time to Complete:	

Lower Body Muscle Groups	Exercise	Reps	Weight (lbs)	Minutes Between Sets	Intensity Level	Reps	Weight (lbs)	Minutes Between Sets	Intensity Level
Quads	2 xT	12	120	1	5	12?	12	1	5
		10	125	1	6	125	10	1	6
		8	125	1	7	125	8	1	9
		6	125	1	8	125	6	1	1
High Point	squats	12	125	0	9	125	12	0	9
		12	90	2	10	9	12	2	8
Hamstrings	curls	12	60	1	5	12	60	1	5
		10	65	1	6	10	65	1	6
		8	70	1	7	8	70	1	7
		6	75	1	8	6	75	1	8
High Point	lunges	12	70	0	9	12	70	0	8
		12	40	2	10	12	40	2	8
Calves	e xT	12	40	1	5	12	40	1	5
		10	45	1	6	10	45	1	6
		8	45	1	7	8	45	1	
		6	45	1	8	6	45	8	
High Point	1 leg	12	45	0	9	12	45	8	
		12	40	2	10	12	40	2	

At this point, you should be 31 minutes into your lower body workout and have 11 minutes to go.

Abs	reverse	12	0	1	5	12	0	1	5
		10	0	1	6	12	0	1	6
	pch	8	0	1	7	12	0	1	9
		6	0	1	8	12	0	1	8
High Point		12	0	0	9	12	0	0	5
		12		–	10	12			0

Notes:

Bill Phillips   Lesson-*for*-LIFE

"You fill your life with what fills your mind."

By this point in the Program you've begun to recognize the tremendous power of your mind to help you achieve the worthwhile objectives you're striving for. In fact, I can virtually guarantee that you've begun to notice that the more optimistic you are—the more excited you become when thinking about how bright your future can be—the more good people and opportunities show up in your life. What I've discovered is that you fill your life with what fills your mind. This is a very important lesson to learn. Unfortunately, many people who are experiencing setbacks, adversity, even failure, don't recognize that the seeds of their misfortune are being planted through unconscious fears, doubts, and negativity that dominate their thoughts. So, please, continue to fill your mind with positive images and feelings of success, and I assure you, *even more* success will fill your life!

Success Story   Lisa Clark

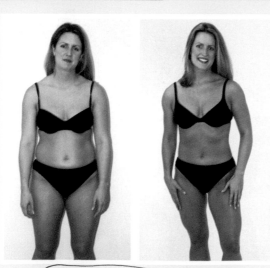

Age 34•Chatham, NJ•Mother
Gained Strength, Lost 15 lbs of Fat

I love this Program! I love being a part of it and sharing it with others. It's so fun to meet people who are doing the Challenge and talk with them about it. Whenever I tell people about Body-*for*-LIFE, I encourage them to take their before photo, set their goals, and make all 12 weeks really count! I'm so glad I accepted this Challenge. My family is really benefiting as well. We are making health a priority in our lives. This has helped me realize how much good health can impact your entire life!

Body-*for*-LIFE   The Power Mindset

Please write down 5 things you can do between now and this time tomorrow
that will help you move forward in the direction of your 12-week goals.

	PLAN	ACTUAL
1		
2		
3		
4		
5		

Body-*for*-LIFE   The Universal Law of Reciprocation

Please write down 2 things you can do between now and
this time tomorrow to support and encourage others.

	PLAN	ACTUAL
1		
2		

Body-*for*-LIFE   Focus on Progress, Not Perfection

Please write down 3 things you did very well today that helped
you move toward the achievement of your 12-week goals.

1	
2	
3	

Please write down one thing you will do even better tomorrow.

1	

Notes:

Body-for-LIFE The Eating-for-LIFE Method™

PLAN		ACTUAL	
Meal 1		**Meal 1**	
☐ a.m. ☐ p.m.		☐ a.m. ☐ p.m.	
Meal 2		**Meal 2**	
☐ a.m. ☐ p.m.		☐ a.m. ☐ p.m.	
Meal 3		**Meal 3**	
☐ a.m. ☐ p.m.		☐ a.m. ☐ p.m.	
Meal 4		**Meal 4**	
☐ a.m. ☐ p.m.		☐ a.m. ☐ p.m.	
Meal 5		**Meal 5**	
☐ a.m. ☐ p.m.		☐ a.m. ☐ p.m.	
Meal 6		**Meal 6**	
☐ a.m. ☐ p.m.		☐ a.m. ☐ p.m.	

Notes:

Body-for-LIFE

The 20-Minute Aerobics Solution™

Intensity Pattern	PLAN		ACTUAL	
	Planned Start Time: 6:33		Actual Start Time: 7:35	
	Planned End Time: 6:0		Actual End Time: 7:55	
	Time to Complete: 20 Minutes		Time to Complete: 20'	

Exercise	Minute by Minute	Intensity Level	Minute by Minute	Intensity Level
	1	5	1	5
	2	5	2	5
	3	6	3	6
	4	7	4	7
P3 level 4	5	8	5	
	6	9	6	8
	7	6	7	9
	8	7	8	5
	9	8	9	6
	10	9	10	7
	11	6	11	8
	12	7	12	9
	13	8	13	5
	14	9	14	6
	15	6	15	7
	16	7	16	8
	17	8	17	9
High Point	18	9	18	9½
	19	10	19	
	20	5	20	5

Notes:

6.02   187 — 170 —1'rs— 151

385 cal

DAY 80

Bill Phillips — Lesson-*for*-LIFE

"When you succeed, we all win."

Although successfully completing a Body-*for*-LIFE transformation appears to be an "individual sport," it's actually not. It's a "team sport." And by that I mean that when you succeed, we all win. The entire Body-*for*-LIFE community celebrates your achievements! And your victory strengthens the entire team. Right now, there are thousands of Body-*for*-LIFE winners cheering you on. We are all pulling for you. We are all on your side! And we support you no matter what your age, gender, or where you're from. The Body-*for*-LIFE community is now worldwide and includes people from Russia, China, Australia, Brazil, Switzerland, Canada, New Zealand, Germany, Spain, Great Britain, Sweden, Iceland, Japan, Greece, Mexico, Thailand, South Africa, Italy, and other places the world over. We are a team. And we care about your success. With each and every person who transforms, this championship team becomes stronger!

Success Story — Robert White

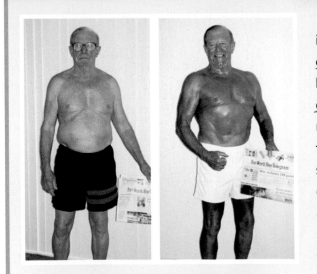

Age 77 • Bedford, TX • Retired USAF Pilot
Gained Energy, Decreased Bodyfat 5%

I was a U.S. Air Force pilot and instructor. I maintained good health over the years, but a bout with cancer hastened my retirement and left me devastated. This Challenge motivated me. At times, it was necessary to continue on discipline alone until my usual strong determination resurfaced. I am extremely gratified to learn my mind and body are capable of accomplishments that a short time ago I would have thought impossible! I'm honored to be among the other winners who have completed this Challenge.

Body-*for*-LIFE The Power Mindset

Please write down 5 things you can do between now and this time tomorrow
that will help you move forward in the direction of your 12-week goals.

	PLAN	ACTUAL
1		
2		
3		
4		
5		

Body-*for*-LIFE The Universal Law of Reciprocation

Please write down 2 things you can do between now and
this time tomorrow to support and encourage others.

	PLAN	ACTUAL
1		
2		

Body-*for*-LIFE Focus on Progress, Not Perfection

Please write down 3 things you did very well today that helped
you move toward the achievement of your 12-week goals.

1	
2	
3	

Please write down one thing you will do even better tomorrow.

1	

Notes:

Body-*for*-LIFE   The Eating-*for*-LIFE Method™

PLAN		ACTUAL	
Meal 1		**Meal 1**	
☐ a.m. ☐ p.m.	myop rx dejvr	☐ a.m. ☐ p.m.	
Meal 2		**Meal 2**	
☐ a.m. ☐ p.m.	mgs n	☐ a.m. ☐ p.m.	
Meal 3		**Meal 3**	
☐ a.m. ☐ p.m.	Merx	☐ a.m. ☐ p.m.	
Meal 4		**Meal 4**	
☐ a.m. ☐ p.m.	Me ə	☐ a.m. ☐ p.m.	
Meal 5		**Meal 5**	
☐ a.m. ☐ p.m.	Frll	☐ a.m. ☐ p.m.	
Meal 6		**Meal 6**	
☐ a.m. ☐ p.m.		☐ a.m. ☐ p.m.	

Notes:

Body-*for*-LIFE — Upper Body Workout

Intensity Pattern

	PLAN		ACTUAL	
Planned Start Time: 7:00			Actual Start Time: _____	
Planned End Time: 7:46			Actual End Time: _____	
Time to Complete: 46 Minutes			Time to Complete: _____	

Upper Body Muscle Groups	Exercise	Reps	Weight (lbs)	Minutes Between Sets	Intensity Level	Reps	Weight (lbs)	Minutes Between Sets	Intensity Level
Chest	incline	12	40	1	5	12	40	1	5
	BP	10	45	1	6	10	45	1	6
	—	8	45	1	7 2:2	8	45	1	7
		6	45	1	8 3.53	6	45	1	8
High Point		12	45	0	9 5.15	12	45	0	9
		12	40	2	10	12	40	2	10
Shoulders	press	12	25	1	5 9.27	12	25	1	5
		10	30	1	6 10.5	10	30	1	6
		8	35	1	7 12.7	8	35	1	7
		6	40	1	8 13.4	6	40	1	8
High Point		12	35	0	9 14.5	12	35	0	9
		12	10	2	10	12	10	2	10
Back	row	12	40	1	5 17.15	12	40	1	5
		10	45	1	6 20.	10	25	1	6
		8	45	1	7 22-10	8	45	1	7
		6	45	1	8 23.5	6	45	1	8
High Point		12	45	0	9	12	45	0	9
	max	12	30 40	2	10	12	45	2	8
Triceps	ext	12	25	1	5 28.3	12	25	1	5
		10	25	1	6	10		1	6
		8	25	1	7	8		1	7
		6	25	1	8	6		1	8
High Point		12	25	0	9	12		0	9
		12	0	2	10	12	3-3	2	8

At this point, you should be 37 minutes into your upper body workout and have 9 minutes to go.

Biceps	curls	12	20	1	5	12	20	5	5
		10	25	1	6 39.45	10	25	6	6
		8	30	1	7 41.1	8	30	7	4
		6	35	1	8 42.8	6	35	8	8
High Point		12	30	0	9 45	12	30	0	
	hammer curl	12	25	—	10	11	25	0	

Notes: _____

_____

_____

Bill Phillips — Lesson-*for*-LIFE

"The way things have 'always been' is not necessarily the way things will always be."

One of the most empowering lessons I've seen so many people learn as they complete the Body-*for*-LIFE Challenge is that *the past does not equal the future*. The way things have "always been" is not necessarily the way things will always be *if* a person decides to make a change *and* follows through. This experience of transforming your health and fitness is an example of the potential you have to change numerous aspects of your life. Today, as you near the completion of this 12-week Body-*for*-LIFE Program, ask yourself, "If I can do this, *what else can I do?*" Realize that you don't have to settle for anything less than what you really want. This experience has taught you that. And you have also learned that you *are* capable of making the commitment and doing the work necessary to change for the better. So ask yourself, "What do I want to transform next?"

Success Story — Russell Simpson, M.D.

Age 47•Huntsville, AL•Physician
Gained 12 lbs of Muscle, Lost 16 lbs of Fat

I had spent years training to become a medical doctor. Outwardly, I had it made. I have a great family, my kids are going to the best school in town, and I live in a house bigger than I need. But one thing I secretly wished for was to be in exceptional shape. So I accepted the Challenge to build my body and find my passion for health again. Within a few weeks, my energy began to surge, and I was sleeping better than I had in a long time. Now I feel good, and I honestly believe there is no mountain too high for me to climb!

Body-*for*-LIFE   The Power Mindset

Please write down 5 things you can do between now and this time tomorrow that will help you move forward in the direction of your 12-week goals.

	PLAN	ACTUAL
1		
2		
3		
4		
5		

Body-*for*-LIFE   The Universal Law of Reciprocation

Please write down 2 things you can do between now and this time tomorrow to support and encourage others.

	PLAN	ACTUAL
1		
2		

Body-*for*-LIFE   Focus on Progress, Not Perfection

Please write down 3 things you did very well today that helped you move toward the achievement of your 12-week goals.

1	
2	
3	

Please write down one thing you will do even better tomorrow.

1	

Notes:

Body-*for*-LIFE The Eating-*for*-LIFE Method™

PLAN		ACTUAL	
Meal 1		**Meal 1**	
☐ a.m. ☐ p.m.		☐ a.m. ☐ p.m.	
Meal 2		**Meal 2**	
☐ a.m. ☐ p.m.		☐ a.m. ☐ p.m.	
Meal 3		**Meal 3**	
☐ a.m. ☐ p.m.		☐ a.m. ☐ p.m.	
Meal 4		**Meal 4**	
☐ a.m. ☐ p.m.		☐ a.m. ☐ p.m.	
Meal 5		**Meal 5**	
☐ a.m. ☐ p.m.		☐ a.m. ☐ p.m.	
Meal 6		**Meal 6**	
☐ a.m. ☐ p.m.		☐ a.m. ☐ p.m.	

Notes:

Body-*for*-LIFE

The 20-Minute Aerobics Solution™

Intensity Pattern

	PLAN		ACTUAL	
Planned Start Time: _C:00_			Actual Start Time: _C:35_	
Planned End Time: _C:2_			Actual End Time: _C:55_	
Time to Complete: 20 Minutes			Time to Complete: _20_	

Exercise	Minute by Minute	Intensity Level	Minute by Minute	Intensity Level
	1	5	1	5
	2	5	2	6
	3	6	3	7
	4	7	4	8
	5	8	5	9
P3 level 5	6	9	6	5
	7	6	7	6
	8	7	8	7
	9	8	9	8
	10	9	10	8
	11	6	11	9
	12	7	12	5
	13	8	13	6
	14	9	14	7
	15	6	15	8
	16	7	16	8
	17	8	17	9
High Point	18	9	18	
	19	10	19	10
	20	5	20	5

Notes:

196 176 — 16

9.96

3459

reached me FIR

Bill Phillips — Lesson-*for*-LIFE

"Your success is giving others hope that
they too have the power to change!"

One of the most inspiring aspects of this journey, which I'm sure you are already experiencing, is that your success is giving others hope that they too have the power to change! Your example is being noticed by more people than you might even realize. You are becoming respected and recognized as a leader.

Success Story — Diane Robertson

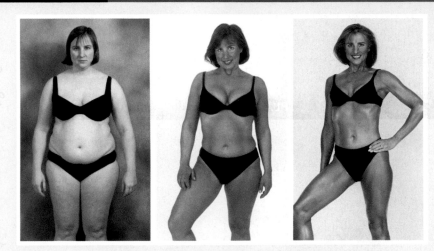

Age 43 • Chatham Township, NJ • Preschool Director
Lost 71 lbs of Fat, Gained Strength

In order to succeed, I had to get out of the comfort zone and enter the war zone. The juggling act was stressful at first, but I knew it had to be a priority for me to succeed. I completed three consecutive rounds of the Program, dropping from a size 18 to a size 2. With the 71 lbs of fat I lost, I also lost 12 inches off my hips, 17 inches off my waist, and almost 10 inches off each leg. My cholesterol dropped from 235 to 158. I have gained the self-respect and self-worth that has empowered me to take on new challenges and opportunities. I have also become involved in helping many others and have set and achieved countless other goals. I've been transformed from follower to leader.

Body-*for*-LIFE   The Power Mindset

Please write down 5 things you can do between now and this time tomorrow that will help you move forward in the direction of your 12-week goals.

	PLAN	ACTUAL
1		
2		
3		
4		
5		

Body-*for*-LIFE   The Universal Law of Reciprocation

Please write down 2 things you can do between now and this time tomorrow to support and encourage others.

	PLAN	ACTUAL
1		
2		

Body-*for*-LIFE   Focus on Progress, Not Perfection

Please write down 3 things you did very well today that helped you move toward the achievement of your 12-week goals.

1	
2	
3	

Please write down one thing you will do even better tomorrow.

1	

Notes:

DAY 82

Body-*for*-LIFE The Eating-*for*-LIFE Method™

PLAN		ACTUAL	
Meal 1		**Meal 1**	
☐ a.m. ☐ p.m.		☐ a.m. ☐ p.m.	
Meal 2		**Meal 2**	
☐ a.m. ☐ p.m.		☐ a.m. ☐ p.m.	
Meal 3		**Meal 3**	
☐ a.m. ☐ p.m.		☐ a.m. ☐ p.m.	
Meal 4		**Meal 4**	
☐ a.m. ☐ p.m.		☐ a.m. ☐ p.m.	
Meal 5		**Meal 5**	
☐ a.m. ☐ p.m.		☐ a.m. ☐ p.m.	
Meal 6		**Meal 6**	
☐ a.m. ☐ p.m.		☐ a.m. ☐ p.m.	

Notes:

Body-for-LIFE — Lower Body Workout

	Intensity Pattern

PLAN	ACTUAL
Planned Start Time: _____	Actual Start Time: 7:02
Planned End Time: _____	Actual End Time: 7:37
Time to Complete: 42 Minutes	Time to Complete: _____

Lower Body Muscle Groups	Exercise	Reps	Weight (lbs)	Minutes Between Sets	Intensity Level	Reps	Weight (lbs)	Minutes Between Sets	Intensity Level
Quads	extension	12	120	1	5	12	120	1	5
		10	125	1	6	10	125	1	6
		8	125	1	7	8	125	1	7
		6	125	1	8 4	6	125	1	8
High Point		12	125	0	9	12	125	6	8
	squats	12	90	2	10	12	90	1	9
Hamstrings	curls	12	60	1	5	12	60	1	5
		10	65	1	6 10.10	10	65	1	6
		8	70	1	7 12	8	70	1	7
		6	75	1	8 13.6	6	75	1	8
High Point		12	70	0	9	12	70	0	9
	lunges	12	40	2	10	12	40	2	9
Calves	2x7	12	40	1	5	12	40	1	5
		10	45	1	6 21	10	45	1	6
		8	45	1	7 22.4	8	45	1	7
		6	45	1	8	6	45	1	6
High Point		12	45	0	9 24.5 12	12	45	5	
	calf	12	40	2	10	12	40	2	

At this point, you should be 31 minutes into your lower body workout and have 11 minutes to go.

Abs	reverse	12	0	1	5	12	0	1	5
	crunch	10	0	1	6	10	0	1	6
		8	0	1	7	8	0	1	7
		6	0	1	8	6	0	1	4
High Point		12	0	0	9	12	0	0	5
	ball	12	0	–	10	12		0	9

Notes: push workout
later finish

Bill Phillips   Lesson-*for*-LIFE

"You did it! You absolutely, positively did it! Congratulations!!"

I am so proud of you! You made the decision to make a change, set your goals, planned and prepared, transformed bad habits into good, and had faith in yourself. You not only worked out, you pushed yourself beyond a level that you had ever experienced before! And you've learned to feed your body with good nutrition, and nourish your mind with good thoughts and ideas. You've also learned that success has little to do with chance and a great deal to do with choice. And the choices you've made have brought you to this point—you have totally transformed! You have become healthier and stronger in so many ways. I encourage you to harness the momentum and positive energy of this experience and continue to improve your body *and* life! Once again... *congratulations* and *welcome* to the Body-*for*-LIFE community of winners!

Success Story   Jaime Brunner

Age 25 • Phoenix, AZ • Restaurant Manager
Gained 5 lbs of Muscle, Lost 20 lbs of Fat

I think the reason I'm so happy now is because I know what it feels like to *not* be happy. I remember what it feels like to be ashamed of my body, to feel trapped under all the fat. I would never go back to the way I was living before. I don't ever want to look like that or feel like that again! Why would anyone come this far and then turn back? I can't think of any reason to not *live* this way. With every person who transforms his or her body, others will follow. It's the greatest thing, and I feel fortunate to be a part of it!

Body-*for*-LIFE — The Power Mindset

Please write down 5 things you can do between now and this time tomorrow
that will help you move forward in the direction of your 12-week goals.

	PLAN	ACTUAL
1		
2		
3		
4		
5		

Body-*for*-LIFE — The Universal Law of Reciprocation

Please write down 2 things you can do between now and
this time tomorrow to support and encourage others.

	PLAN	ACTUAL
1		
2		

Body-*for*-LIFE — Focus on Progress, Not Perfection

Please write down 3 things you did very well today that helped
you move toward the achievement of your 12-week goals.

1	
2	
3	

Please write down one thing you will do even better tomorrow.

1	

Notes:

Body-*for*-LIFE | The Eating-*for*-LIFE Method™

PLAN		ACTUAL	
Meal 1		**Meal 1**	
☐ a.m. ☐ p.m.		☐ a.m. ☐ p.m.	
Meal 2		**Meal 2**	
☐ a.m. ☐ p.m.		☐ a.m. ☐ p.m.	
Meal 3		**Meal 3**	
☐ a.m. ☐ p.m.		☐ a.m. ☐ p.m.	
Meal 4		**Meal 4**	
☐ a.m. ☐ p.m.		☐ a.m. ☐ p.m.	
Meal 5		**Meal 5**	
☐ a.m. ☐ p.m.		☐ a.m. ☐ p.m.	
Meal 6		**Meal 6**	
☐ a.m. ☐ p.m.		☐ a.m. ☐ p.m.	

Notes:

Body-*for*-LIFE | The 20-Minute Aerobics Solution™

Intensity Pattern

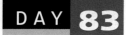

Exercise	PLAN		ACTUAL	
	Planned Start Time: _____		**Actual Start Time:** _____	
	Planned End Time: _____		**Actual End Time:** _____	
	Time to Complete: 20 Minutes		**Time to Complete:** _____	
	Minute by Minute	Intensity Level	Minute by Minute	Intensity Level
	1	5	1	5
	2	5	2	6
	3	6	3	7
	4	7	4	8
	5	8	5	9
	6	9	6	
	7	6	7	5
	8	7	8	6
	9	8	9	7
	10	9	10	8
	11	6	11	
	12	7	12	9
	13	8	13	5
	14	9	14	
	15	6	15	6
	16	7	16	7
	17	8	17	1
↳ **High Point**	18	9	18	9
	19	10	19	9
	20	5	20	5

Notes: 181 — 160 — 150

350